Twayne's English Authors Series

EDITOR OF THIS VOLUME

Kinley E. Roby

Northeastern University

T.E. Lawrence

TEAS 233

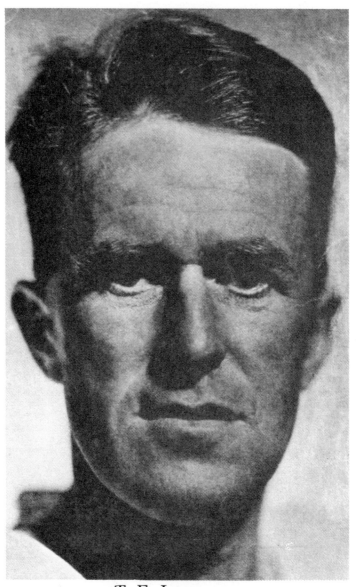

T. E. Lawrence

T. E. LAWRENCE

By STEPHEN ELY TABACHNICK

Ben-Gurion University of the Negev

TWAYNE PUBLISHERS
A DIVISON OF G. K. HALL & CO. BOSTON

Library of Congress Cataloging in Publication Data

Tabachnick, Stephen Ely.
  T. E. Lawrence.

  (Twayne's English authors series; TEAS 233)
  Bibliography: p. 157-65
  Includes index.
  1. Lawrence, Thomas Edward, 1888-1935—Criticism and
interpretation.
PR6023.A937Z88   828'.9'1208   77-18244
ISBN 0-8057-6704-5

PR
6023
.A937
Z88

71629

To Rex Warner,
the only kind genius I have ever met

Contents

About the Author

Educated at the Universities of Berkeley, Chicago and Connecticut, S. E. Tabachnick received his doctorate in 1971 and has taught at the Ben-Gurion University of the Negev and the Hebrew University, Jerusalem. He is currently Senior Lecturer and Chairman of the Department of English at the Ben-Gurion University. Although Dr. Tabachnick specializes in T. E. Lawrence and the literature of British imperialism, particularly Anglo-Arabian travel writing, he has co-authored *Harold Pinter* (1973) and has published articles on a wide range of British and American literature.

Preface

Praised extravagantly by Thomas Hardy, George Bernard Shaw, and E. M. Forster (upon whose *A Passage to India* it exerted a direct influence), T. E. Lawrence's *Seven Pillars of Wisdom* today suffers from a lack of critical attention and remains outside the university literature curriculum. Because the book seemingly straddles the genres of autobiography, history, travel writing, and fiction, it has created complicated problems of interpretation and has been the source of wide critical disagreement since it appeared half a century ago. *Seven Pillars* mirrors the involutions and complexities of Lawrence's life in Arabia and frequently forces extraliterary interpretation; it is as strange and subtle as its main character. However, Lawrence the writer is even more interesting than Lawrence of Arabia, and my method throughout this study has been to use his life to illuminate his books, and not vice versa. As the author of *Seven Pillars* and *The Mint,* the translator of Homer's *Odyssey,* and the compiler of the poetry anthology *Minorities,* Lawrence presents us with a powerful claim for consideration as a "writer of magnitude," as R. P. Blackmur called him.

Eschewing any attempt to psychoanalyze the man Lawrence from his work, this study analyzes *Seven Pillars of Wisdom* as a work of art by definitively identifying its genre and then assessing its structure and style and literary merit according to a coherent theory of autobiography. Thus I avoid the errors of earlier critics who try to squeeze *Seven Pillars* into a novelistic or historical straitjacket which simply does not fit. As an introduction to the formal analysis, I show Lawrence's debt to the nineteenth-century Anglo-Arabian travel book tradition, and reveal the contradictions in his view of love, death, and heroism which come up throughout *Seven Pillars.* A discussion of the many texts of *Seven Pillars* and their relative accuracy and artistic worth leads to a view of Lawrence as a sincere poetic autobiographer and prepares the reader for a detailed analysis of the conflict between his British and Arab identities that informs all of *Seven Pillars*. By tracing carefully this process of mind which Lawrence underwent in Arabia, we come to understand his position as narrator and protagonist in the literature of twentieth-century British imperialism. With Joseph Conrad and Forster, he takes his place as a poet of the conflict of cultures.

A formal analysis of the entire structure of *Seven Pillars*, including the military plot line, and of Lawrence's method of characterization and his many styles, allows us to assess Lawrence's book as a highly successful poetic autobiography. Similarly, an analysis of *The Mint* reveals the successful conclusion of Lawrence's spiritual journey in the form of a bold but failed experiment in autobiographical form. The study begins with a look at the influences which acted on Lawrence the artist; it concludes with a look at the writers whom he, in his turn, influenced, particularly Wilfred Thesiger, whose great *Arabian Sands* owes much to Lawrence.

A French revival of Lawrence as a writer that took place in the 1950s under the distinguished auspices of André Malraux and Jean Beraud Villars failed to reinstate Lawrence. The present Anglo-American effort of Thomas J. O'Donnell, Jeffrey Meyers, Stanley and Rodelle Weintraub, J. M. Wilson, and others—as well as work now going forward in France and Germany—has better chances for success because the majority of these scholars has chosen to specialize in T. E. Lawrence studies and because, as an advertisement of 1975 puts the matter succinctly, "Everybody loves camels, now!" I hope that this study makes Lawrence available to readers, students, and critics who have been either unwilling or unable to recognize his virtues as a writer. The new Lawrence revival is still gathering strength, and this book will add, hopefully, to its momentum. Lawrence, whose love of speed led to his death on a motorcycle, might watch this growing movement with the satisfaction of a man fast coming into his own.

STEPHEN ELY TABACHNICK

Ben-Gurion University of the Negev

Acknowledgments

I am obliged to J. M. Wilson, the Lawrence Trustees and Doubleday and Co. for permission to quote from unpublished and published material, including *Seven Pillars of Wisdom* and *The Mint;* and to Jonathan Cape, Ltd. and the Letters Trust for T. E. Lawrence for permission to quote from the *Letters.* Helmut Gerber, editor of *English Literature in Transition: 1880*–1920; Stephen Goode, editor of *Studies in the Twentieth Century;* and Henry Grosshans, editor of *Research Studies*, kindly allowed me to reprint in somewhat different form material from my articles, which are listed in the bibliography; parts of Chapters 2, 5, and 7 have appeared in these articles.

I am indebted to my few colleagues in the Lawrence field, particularly Jeffrey Meyers, Thomas O'Donnell, J. M. Wilson, and Stanley and Rodelle Weintraub, for granting me deeper understanding of an extremely complicated subject; and to librarians at the Houghton Library, the Bodleian Library, Jesus College (Oxford), the British Library, the University of Connecticut, and the Ben-Gurion University of the Negev for very gracious treatment. I also wish to thank the Harvard Library which has granted me permission to publish terms from its manuscript holdings.

Dr. William Baker, Dr. Zev Bar-Lev and Dr. Jay Shir contributed suggestions which were really helpful, as did Professors William Moynihan, Joseph Cary and Paul Alkon. I thank Professor Shalom J. Kahn of the Hebrew University for suggesting that I teach a course in American autobiography and the students in that course, as well as those in the course on the clash of cultures in modern British literature at the Hebrew and Ben-Gurion Universities, for the opportunity of hearing their ideas and forcing them to hear mine.

I thank Professor Kinley E. Roby for valuable editing. My wife Sharona receives my deepest gratitude for criticism, stylistic corrections, and proofreading. Almost needless to say, I also thank my parents, without whom the whole show, such as it is, would not have been possible.

Chronology

1888   T. E. Lawrence born August 16 at Tremadoc, Wales.

1896–   Attends Oxford High School for Boys.
1907

1907   Attends Jesus College, Oxford; B. A. thesis entitled
1910   *Crusader Castles* (published 1936). Receives Magdalen College travelling scholarship.

1911–   Excavations at Carchemish, Syria with D. G. Hogarth and
1914   C. Leonard Woolley of the Ashmolean Museum result in the coauthored *Carchemish: Report on the Excavations at Djerabis on Behalf of the British Museum* (published 1914, 1921, 1952). Work around Beersheba with Hogarth and Woolley results in coauthored *The Wilderness of Zin* (published 1915).

1911   Writes *Diary of a Journey Across the Euphrates* (published 1937); translates *Two Arabic Tales* (published 1937).

1914–   Military intelligence in Cairo.
1916

1916   Joins Emir Feisal's forces in the field.

1916–   Compiles poetry anthology *Minorities* (published 1971).
1927

1917   November 20; tortured at Deraa.

1915–   War diaries (unpublished).
1918

1916–   Contributions to intelligence newsletter, the *Arab Bulletin*
1918   (Lawrence's contributions published as *Secret Despatches from Arabia*, 1939).

1919   January–August, peace conference in Paris as Feisal's adviser. January 10–July 25, writes Text I of *Seven Pillars of Wisdom;* November, loses it at Reading Station.

1919–   December 2–May 11, writes Text II of *Seven Pillars of*
1920   *Wisdom.* (Destroys it May 10, 1922, except for specimen page preserved in Text III.)

1919–   Fellow, All Souls College, Oxford.
1920

1920– 1922	September 1–May 9, writes Text III.
1921– 1922	January–July, adviser to Winston Churchill in the Colonial Office.
1922	January 20–June 24, "Oxford text" of *Seven Pillars of Wisdom.*
1922	August, joins Royal Air Force under name John Hume Ross.
1922– 1928	Composes *The Mint* (published 1955).
1923	January, discharged from Royal Air Force. February, joins Royal Tank Corps under name T. E. Shaw.
1924	Publishes translation of Le Corbeau's *Le Gigantesque (The Forest Giant).*
1925	Rejoins Royal Air Force.
1926	Subscriber's Edition of *Seven Pillars of Wisdom.*
1927	*Revolt in the Desert,* an abridgement of *Seven Pillars of Wisdom.* Posted to India.
1928– 1931	Translates Homer's *Odyssey* (published 1934).
1933	"A Handbook to the 37½ Foot Motor Boats of the 200 Class."
1935	February 26, retires from the Royal Air Force. May 13, fatally injured in motorcycle accident near Clouds Hill, Dorset. May 19, death of T. E. Lawrence.
1938	*The Letters of T. E. Lawrence.*
1940	*Men in Print: Essays in Literary Criticism.*

CHAPTER 1

Introduction

I Critical Review

M OST travelers who enter Beersheba on the old road from Tel Aviv probably fail to notice the old Hejaz Railway station and companion water tower which merges unwillingly into the background of modern apartment houses on the right side of the road; they speed by the British military cemetary one hundred yards farther over to the right and do not see the more than one thousand tombstones adorned with romantic and patriotic mottoes of a past age, "In God We Trust," "So Far From Home." If they go through the town center, the old Turkish mosque and administration buildings look to them like natural aspects of a landscape which contains many old mosques and buildings; the twelve foot high obelisk with "ALLENBY 1917-1918" engraved on it never appears to their eyes, obscured by trees and automobile exhaust. When they leave the town headed for Eilat, the arched old railway bridge over Wadi Beersheba is only a blur.

Today's travelers and busy town of 100,000 inhabitants have their own wars and their own monuments, and no time for remnants of vanished colonial battles, including the one which took place from 6:00 A.M. to 6:00 P.M. on October 31, 1917, at Beersheba, involved forty thousand men, and ended only when the Fourth Australian Light Horse Regiment managed to gallop the Turkish defenses on the Hebron Road in one of the last great cavalry charges. But the sensitive observer gently transcends the present by peering through the blank eye of the empty water tower and remembers that Beersheba was the first town in Palestine to be captured by the British during World War I; and that far to the east of General Allenby's triumphal flank the very unusual man known as "Lawrence of Arabia" operated in the desolate Arabian and Syrian deserts: the

15

man who made his mark by destroying the same Hejaz Railway (if a different branch than that which ran through Beersheba) and by leaving his literary monuments to these and subsequent adventures, the books known as *Seven Pillars of Wisdom*[1] and *The Mint*[2]. What does the sensitive reader of the first, and by far the greatest, of these books find in it?

To the reader confronting *Seven Pillars of Wisdom* for the first time, it appears a strange book which speaks of alien lands and events with an unusual and unsettling power. The uninitiated reader need not feel embarrassed: the more one studies the man and the book that reflects his personality to such a high degree, the more one feels the presence of an essential mystery. For Lawrence's book conceals at least as much as it reveals about his mental composition and his life in Arabia.

Who was the mysterious "S. A." to whom Lawrence dedicated his book? Why did he feel that "the citadel of my integrity had been irrevocably lost" after his mortifying experience at Deraa? Why does military victory continually engender in him the bitterness of defeat? What is the meaning of his abrupt shifts in sympathy toward both British and Arabs? Most of all, what shape of personality can we assign to this erratic poetic autobiographer? Even after half a century, these questions remain largely unanswered, although dedicated scholars have begun to construct a reliable picture.

Lawrence's greatest book, seen as a literary work of art, reflects these mysteries of its content, and continues to excite debate and disagreement among its critics. Only recently have literary critics proven somewhat more able to agree on the book's essential merit and final place in literature than Lawrence's biographers who, grappling with the puzzles of his life, have not yet been able to sum up the man. The history of Lawrence criticism appears as a collage of diametrically opposed views, and Lawrence has not yet achieved a solid position in the canon.

Lawrence reveled in the confusion he sowed among his contemporary critics and biographers. The following extract from a letter he wrote to H. H. Banbury in 1927 after the appearance of his popular abridgement of *Seven Pillars*, entitled *Revolt in the Desert*,[3] testifies to the reigning consternation of the critics and Lawrence's delight in that consternation. And it must be remembered that *Revolt in the Desert* relates the strictly military side of Lawrence's adventures, making it far easier to judge than the more involuted and complex parent work.

Yes, I was sent the Woolf review: and laughed. Here are the judgements of the great upon my style.

'So imitative of Doughty as to be near parody.' Woolf in the *Nation*.

'Has none of Doughty's biblical or Elizabethan anachronisms.' John Buchan in *Sat. Review*.

'Gnarled texture twisted with queer adjective and adverbs.' Woolf.

'Effortless, artless-seeming, adequate prose.' Gerald Bullett.

'Obscure to the point of affectation.' *Tatler*.

'Writing as easy, confident and unselfconscious as a duck's swimming.' *Lit. Digest*.

'Style has a straightforward fierceness, an intrepid directness.' Ellis Roberts.

'Style is like music.' C. F. G. Masterman.

'A scholar's style, simple, direct, free from ornament.' H. W. Nevinson. (*Manch. Guard.*)

'Style here and there affectedly abrupt and strenuous, but mostly without affectation.' Edw. Shanks.

'A cool distinguished prose.' Eric Sutton in *Outlook*.

'Positively breezy.' G. B. Shaw in *Spectator*. There y'are! Take your pick! I wash my hands of the affair: though I protest I am not peevish, as Woolf says.[4]

Until recently, the confusion became greater instead of less. For R. P. Blackmur, writing in 1940, "Except Swift, Lawrence is the least abiding writer of magnitude in English. . . . "[5] In 1955, Richard Aldington finds in *Seven Pillars* a "kind of verbal dodging" that is "the virtue of a politican and intriguer, not of a writer," and concludes that Lawrence "might have written much better if he had not striven so painfully to write too well."[6] Malcolm Muggeridge writes in 1961 that ". . . I found, and find it unreadable, while admiring the care and assiduity with which it has been put together."[7] Stanley Weintraub, in 1963, concludes that "*Seven Pillars of Wisdom*—as literature—does not approach so great a work as the *Iliad*, but rather has the inaccuracies, extravagances, diffuseness, artificiality—and sustained genius for language—of a Miltonic epic, misplaced in time. . . ."[8] Although Weintraub's *Private Shaw and Public Shaw* contains perceptive literary work, it falls primarily into the class of biography rather than criticism.

Only in 1970, forty-five years after the appearance of *Seven Pillars*, did someone find it worthy of the application of modern critical tools of analysis and full-scale treatment. Thomas J. O'Donnell's excellent dissertation[9] represents the pioneering attempt to see Lawrence's work—including *The Mint*—as art and to assign it to a tradition. Preferring the 1922 Oxford text of *Seven Pillars* to the final edition of

1926 because the earlier text reveals more of the "dichotomy of self" in Lawrence, O'Donnell sees the book as "a radical and late representative of the nineteenth-century literature of self-division" which "bears affinities to the works of the *fin-de siécle* aesthetes whom Lawrence admired."[10]

A second dissertation, which has been absorbed into the present work, appeared in 1971 and presented Lawrence as one of the great writers of the century, eschewing a Northrop Frye-like reluctance to make qualitative judgments and displaying the bad taste to call a spade a spade. Fortunately, the same straightforward admiration informs the next full-length work to appear on Lawrence, Jeffrey Meyers' *The Wounded Spirit: A Study of "Seven Pillars of Wisdom"* (London, 1973), which begins by classifying *Seven Pillars* as "essentially and primarily a literary work of genius, beauty and insight . . . a masterpiece of psychological analysis and self-revelation, and" one of "the finest books of the modern age." Meyers' book contains, among other things, excellent comparisons of Lawrence and Nietzsche, Tolstoy and Doughty. The fact that Lawrence is worthy of comparisons on this scale is borne out by G. Wilson Knight's citation of Byron in his 1971 essay on the author of *Seven Pillars*,[11] and John S. Friedman's recent dissertation on Lawrence and Malraux.[12] With this new concurrence on Lawrence's stature as a writer—seen also in Stanley and Rodelle Weintraub's *Lawrence of Arabia* (1975)—and J. M. Wilson's and John Mack's work on the official biography, can assured recognition be far off?

In recognizing Lawrence for what he is—a great writer—contemporary critics will only be seconding the judgment of the recognized artists—as opposed to litterateurs—of Lawrence's own period. To D. G. Hogarth, Lawrence writes that "Hardy read the thing lately, & made me proud with what he said of it" (*L*, 429). George Bernard Shaw wrote in a preface to the exhibition catalog of illustrations from *Seven Pillars* that "it happened that Lawrence's genius included literary genius . . . and the result was a masterpiece of literature."[13] In *Abinger Harvest*, E. M. Forster says about Lawrence and his major book that "he was so modest that he never grasped its greatness, or admitted that he had given something unique to our literature."[14] In *Lawrence and the Arabs*, Robert Graves finds that "*Seven Pillars of Wisdom* is, beyond dispute, a great book. . . ."[15]

On December 6, 1923, Siegfried Sassoon declares in a letter to Lawrence: "I feel ashamed of all these superlatives, but you've worn me down and swept me away, & I *know* the achievement to be great."[16] And Lawrence's letter of election to the Irish Academy of Letters was written by no one less than W. B. Yeats.[17]

The Mint, which contains the far less exciting story of the Royal Air Force sequel to Lawrence's Arabian adventures and is written in a correspondingly austere style, excited from the start an even more mixed reaction than the earlier book and provides a much less secure basis for its author's literary reputation. Forster's judgment of 1928 that "*The Mint* is not as great a work as *The Seven Pillars* either in colour or form"[18] has been echoed by later critics. In a 1955 radio talk, L. P. Hartley declared *The Mint* a failed masterpiece whose artistry was constricted by a too strict style.[19] Referring to the fact that *The Mint* was released for general circulation only in 1955, twenty years after its author's death, V. S. Pritchett calls it "one of those time bombs of literature which fail to go off when the hour comes." He finds it "arty" in the bad sense and its author a "word prig." At the same moment, he enjoys the third section of the book and admits "Lawrence wrote spiritedly about action. Another virtue of *The Mint* lies in its honest effort to get to the bottom of his subject."[20] And despite his enthusiasm for *Seven Pillars*, Jeffrey Meyers neglects *The Mint* almost completely.

Yet the book has not been without its admirers, as letters to Lawrence from Forster, Edward Garnett, and David Garnett, among others, show.[21] The anonymous critic for *Kirkus* has summed up the book's ambivalent appeal better than perhaps anyone else: "The imaginative interpretation, poignant, bitter, devastating, suggests a writer's notebook. And yet at times there's the linear, introspective aspect of a modern novel. Now monotonous, now holding, it is a unique reading experience."[22] The present writer, who once felt that *The Mint* remains on the level of an exercise in journalism despite some powerful passages, has on subsequent readings come around to the opinion of the above reviewer: though of much slighter spiritual and artistic magnitude than *Seven Pillars*, its sequel constitutes a failed but wholly worthy and original literary experiment and deserves attention as such. And since its third section presents a solution to problems raised in *Seven Pillars*, no consideration of Lawrence's mind and art can be complete without it.

II *Life and Career*

Lawrence's life was as unique as his contribution to literature. Thomas Edward Lawrence was born on August 18, 1888, to Thomas Robert Chapman and the former Sarah Madden. Chapman deserted a first wife to elope with Sarah from his home in County Meath, Ireland, and came to England, where he changed his name by deed poll to Lawrence. T. E., the second of five sons, was born at Tremadoc, Wales. The fact of his parents' bigamous relation and assumed name caused him pain all his life, and partially explains why he found it so easy to change his own name to Ross and then Shaw, and why Liddell Hart's biography, 'T. E. Lawrence': in Arabia and After (1964), includes quotation marks around Lawrence's name in the title. The relationship between Lawrence's parents appears to approximate that of Paul Morel's parents in D. H. Lawrence's Sons and Lovers: a strongly Calvinistic mother tames and breaks a freer, more Dionysiac father. No doubt some part of Lawrence's internal civil war and his lifelong celibacy can be traced to this source. On the other hand, D. H. Lawrence's very different path after a similar beginning reveals that we cannot account for T. E.'s very complex personality in this simple way.

Despite Lawrence's felt social handicap, his natural gifts brought him success from the start. From 1896 to 1907, he attended the Oxford High School for Boys, where he made rapid academic progress. He reserved his major interest, the typically English pursuits of medieval military archeology, brass rubbing, and coin collecting, for the hours after school, which bored him. This interest early brought him friendship with C. Leonard Woolley and D. G. Hogarth, official archeologists at the great Ashmolean Museum—which exhibited in 1974 among medieval treasures of the type which attracted the boy Lawrence, relics of Lawrence's own adventures, including his Arab dagger and robe.

During T. E.'s years at Oxford (1907–1910), Hogarth became a trusted mentor who encouraged an interest in the Arabic language and the Near East. In the summer holidays of 1906, 1907, and 1908, Lawrence toured French castles in order to observe their military design. Always one for physical tests of himself, and addicted to sports from his youth, he carried through in the summer of 1909 a solo walking tour of parts of what are now Lebanon, Syria, and Israel in order to gather firsthand information on the incredible castles built by the Crusaders in their kingdom. He consolidated the results of all trips in his beautifully self-illustrated and highly perceptive undergraduate honors thesis, Crusader Castles (2 vols., London, 1936), which presents a novel, if incorrect, theory of architectural history and influence during the period of the Crusades, that the West influenced the East. Later, Lawrence was to learn just how powerful the East's influence could be.

After graduation, Lawrence worked under Hogarth at a dig in Carchemish for three years. From December, 1910, to August, 1914, Lawrence was in Syria for all but seven months. He owed his familiarity with Arab ways to this experience, and it was here that he met Dahoum, the Arab servant who is mentioned once in *Seven Pillars*, and who seems to be the elusive "S. A." according to the most recent inconclusive, if convincing, evidence. In January, 1914, Lawrence and Hogarth joined Woolley at Beersheba for a survey of the desert, including its Nabataean and Byzantine ruins, which resulted in the publication of *The Wilderness of Zin* (1915), the most authoritative source, despite its inaccuracies, on its subject until the appearance of Nelson Glueck's *Rivers in the Desert*. The long-term value of this book by Woolley, Hogarth, and Lawrence was exceeded by its use as a cover for the intelligence work of spying on the Turks and Germans and their Hejaz Railway which the three men were in fact carrying out. Another semiliterary result of this period is *Carchemish: Report on the Excavations at Djerabis on Behalf of the British Museum* (1914, 1921, 1952), also coauthored with Woolley.

World War I began on August 4, 1914; after a brief sojourn in England, Lawrence took his place in the military intelligence service operating out of Cairo. During this period, he took part in the attempt to buy off Khalil Pasha, whose army surrounded ten thousand British troops in Kut, in what is now Iraq. The attempt failed, but Lawrence saw at first hand the military bungling which also resulted in the British catastrophe at Gallipoli. It is no wonder that Lawrence later idolized the new commander-in-chief, General Allenby, once the latter had proven his competence, although Lawrence shows a consistent desire to look up to certain "father figures" throughout his life. Lawrence's major thinking during the Cairo period, which lasted until he joined the Arab forces in October, 1916, was directed toward outwitting the French, then in rivalry with the English for future hegemony in the Near East, as Lawrence saw quite clearly from the start.

When he transferred to the Arab Bureau, a branch of the intelligence service concerned exclusively with Arab affairs, particularly with the revolt of the Sherif of Mecca against the Turks, Lawrence came into direct contact with the Arab Revolt itself. The "Introduction: Foundations of Arab Revolt" of *Seven Pillars* provides us with the religious and political background of the revolt, and explains how Lawrence transferred to the Arab Bureau in order to get himself involved in it. The section ends with Lawrence preparing to take a trip down to Jidda with Ronald Storrs, the Oriental secretary, in order to assess the chances for the revolt's success. "Book I" of *Seven Pillars* tells of Lawrence's first visit to Arabia, his meeting with the Sherif of Mecca and his three sons, Abdulla, Zeid, and Feisal, and his choice of Feisal as the man to lead the revolt with English backing. Lawrence's full involvement has not yet begun, and his tone is cool and lighthearted. The second book details Lawrence's appointment as Feisal's adviser, his donning of Arab dress, and his invention of the tactic of railway attack and guerrilla warfare in place of more conventional methods of war. Feisal moves his base from Yenbo up the coast to Wejh. In "Book III," particularly the brilliant Chapter 33, Lawrence develops his theory of guerrilla warfare fully. Instead of attacking the Turks entrenched at Medina, Lawrence advocates wide deployment, raiding tactics, and preaching to the tribes to enlist idealistic support. He tries his tactics on the railroad with partial success. Auda abu Tayi, the Homeric Beduin desert fighter, enters the picture, and Lawrence and he work out a brilliant plan of attack on Akaba, far to the north at the end of the Red Sea. The next book, one of the military climaxes of *Seven Pillars,* recounts the epic march through several hundred miles of desert to the final victorious charge on Akaba. Akaba having been taken, "Book V" demonstrates the increased importance of the Arab forces as Allenby's right flank. Lawrence polishes his railway techniques, and the book closes with a successful raid. He has gradually progressed from an adviser and observer to one of the principal actors of the revolt, and the tone of his writing begins to darken.

"Book VI" constitutes Lawrence's dark night of the soul. Not only does a raid on the bridges over the Yarmuk River fail after the exertion and expectation of a long march, but he is personally captured by the Turks at Deraa and tortured. This torture, described vaguely and mysteriously in Chapter 80, has a profoundly depressing effect on his spirit and leads in the direction of nihilism and disillusionment. Yet, at the end of the book, Lawrence is standing by Allenby's side in captured Jerusalem: personal failure and Allied success form a grim counterpoint. In "Book VII," a misunderstanding with the Emir Zeid leads Lawrence to attempt quitting the Arab Movement altogether; but General Allenby sends him back to Feisal. "Book VIII" is another "waiting" section, in which Lawrence's forces lay seige to Maan's Turkish garrison and concentrate on cutting the railway. Lawrence receives over two thousand camels from Allenby and prepares for an attack on the Deraa sector, ever closer to the goal of Damascus. Although he acts, he tells us that he wishes to quit the movement entirely. In the next section, plans for the northward thrust continue, and Lawrence cynically discusses himself and the egoistic reality underlying the heroic ideal. By the time Damascus is reached on October 1, 1918, the Arabs' heroic cries of victory are undercut by Lawrence's personal estrangement from them and from the British. The whole story closes on this note of triumphant military climax and personal despair.

Liddell Hart praises Lawrence as one of the originators of modern guerrilla warfare, including the doctrine of the indirect attack and high mobility and firepower, and Douglas Orgill, in the *Lawrence* volume of "Ballantine's Illustrated History of the Violent Century" (1973), repeats this praise, if in a modified form. On the other hand, Richard Aldington's debunking of Lawrence extends to his military prowess, which he denies almost completely. We are not concerned with Lawrence's military ability in this study, except as it relates to his heroic or antiheroic vision in *Seven Pillars*. Still, it seems worthwhile to consider this aspect here if nowhere else because it does impinge on the truth content of Lawrence's autobiography. Michael Bograd, a soldier in the British army in World War II and now an officer in the Israeli army, concludes a sixty-page study of Lawrence as guerrilla commander with a balanced judgment: Lawrence's way of using the Beduin was correct, and at Tafileh he showed a "good grasp of military tactics." Also, his flexibility in action saved lives and his adherence to the objective of taking Damascus and installing Feisal as king there is exemplary. However, "To conclude from his conduct of small military actions, some of them crassly unsuccessful, that he had the makings of a great commander would be presumptuous."[23] This neutral conclusion, which regards Lawrence as a potentially brilliant but untried military leader, is based on a reading of *Seven Pillars* itself, and thus demonstrates Lawrence's essential sincerity in recounting failures as well as military successes.

As our synopsis has indicated, in addition to the story of Lawrence's military command, *Seven Pillars* records the severe conflict of roles he experienced during the adventure, and his profound bitterness over its spiritual and political outcome.

The bitterness stems in part from his position as Feisal's adviser during the Versailles Peace Conference of 1919, in which he watched

France gain control over Syria despite promises made to Feisal by himself and the British government, which as mandatory power would probably have granted the Arabs a far greater degree of independence than France was prepared to give. The writing of *Seven Pillars* also took its toll. He began writing the book in Paris in January, 1919, lost a first draft, and continued writing and rewriting it until 1926, taking it through five manuscripts in the process. During the early years home, he wrote at the prodigious rate of four or five thousand words a day, and once finished thirty-four thousand words in twenty-four hours, if we take his word for it. The strain of reliving through his writing tortured experiences, a self-imposed physical privation, and the results of an air crash in 1919, often brought him near the edge of madness. His precarious balance notwithstanding, he became an adviser to Winston Churchill in the Colonial Office in January, 1921, and by July, 1922, when he resigned, could declare himself satisfied that England had fulfilled her promises to the Arabs by placing Abdullah on the throne of Transjordan and Feisal in control of Iraq.

Ironically, at the same time he approached a nervous breakdown from 1919 on, Lawrence became a popular hero owing to the efforts of Lowell Thomas, an American journalist commissioned to broadcast Allied efforts during the war. Even more ironically, Thomas' exaggerated portrait of Lawrence—which its subject publicly scorned—grew directly out of T. E.'s desire to be the object of such a portrait. As Thomas tells us,[24] Lawrence proved only too eager to play the role of "Lawrence of Arabia," and came to see the show five times! Here we see Lawrence in only one of his many contradictory aspects: an almost pathological shyness concerning his mental life and a powerful desire for the public spotlight. Lawrence's favorite method of preserving his privacy consisted of weaving a maze of contradictory stories about himself, a method that permitted him to realize both his desires at once. At the same time, it should be noted that he deliberately left behind manuscripts from which a reliable picture of himself and the events in which he was involved may be constructed, if with very great difficulty.

As a cure for his undefined spiritual malaise, he joined the Royal Air Force in August, 1922, under the name John Hume Ross. In January, 1923, he was discharged upon the discovery by reporters that the famous Colonel Lawrence of Arabia was serving in the R.A.F. as a mere private. *The Mint,* composed between 1922 and

1928 and not published until after his death, offers a detailed account of his life as a recruit. In "Part One: The Raw Material," the reader follows a nervous Lawrence from the outside of the recruiting station, through the preliminary medical examination and all the humiliations of drilling, fatigue duty, and foolish officers. The harsh portrait of his wounded commanding officer given in Chapter 20 focusses all his resentment of basic training. The only question that remains unanswered is precisely why Lawrence willingly submitted himself to this treatment. "Part Two: In the Mill" describes the next stage of training, the "square," in which the men are formed into a coherent unit. Lawrence offers close descriptions of the personalities of his buddies and of their life together, but admits in Chapter 19 at the end of this section that he is "Odd Man Out," not really integrated into his company. The final part, "Service," takes place three years after the ending of "square" duty, and finds Lawrence happy and at ease in the R.A.F. Cadet College. He feels at one with the other men, with his work, and with nature and life itself. In this section of the book, Lawrence solves the spiritual problems that he had not resolved in *Seven Pillars* or the first two parts of *The Mint*. In *The Mint*, Lawrence's personality is embodied in a new form of autobiography, a unique artistic achievement. During this period Lawrence also found time to translate Adrien Le Corbeau's *Le Gigantesque*, the record of the growth of a redwood tree, into English, and to write many articles and letters to newspapers and friends. His vast lifetime correspondence, available in thick volumes, reveals a deep sensitivity and real epistolary talent.

A month after being dismissed from the air force, Lawrence reenlisted in the Tank Corps under the name T. E. Shaw. He withstood the harsh life of the "Tanks" for more than two years, but in August, 1925, succeeded in getting himself retransferred to the R.A.F., his true enthusiasm. While serving in the R.A.F. in India, he produced for Bruce Rogers a translation of the *Odyssey* (New York 1934) almost as interesting and original as his translator's preface, which attacks Homer as a man and as a writer. The great classics scholar Maurice Bowra, in his own introduction to Lawrence's translation, accepts some of Lawrence's criticisms of the *Odyssey* but sees through them to Lawrence's genuine admiration for the Greek poet, and praises Lawrence's special gift:

But when we set his translation against others, two qualities seem to emerge

and give it a special distinction. The first is that he enjoys the story for its own sake and spares nothing to keep it clear and lively, to make the details illuminate and strengthen the whole effect and never to allow the plot to be lost in undue emphasis on the wrong point. The second is that he sees the whole Homeric world with a clear vision as Homer himself saw it. (*The Odyssey of Homer*, trans. T. E. Shaw, with an intro. by Sir Maurice Bowra, London, 1955, p. xvi).

Lawrence's lifelong interest in Homer's work contributed to his vision of the Beduin in life and art, and his experience with them in Arabia helped him with his translation. However, even in the relative retirement of India his scholarly peace was shattered by fantastic newspaper reports of espionage activities, and in January, 1929, he was ordered back to England.

From his return until just before his death on May 19, 1935, he remained in the R.A.F., leading a life idyllic in its numbness but becoming a good mechanic in the process, as his "Handbook to the 37½ Foot Motor Boats of the 200 Class" (1933) testifies. His brain and erudition never dulled, and to the last he remained sensitive to the arts, particularly literature and music, and intimate with some of the best minds in England. He was fatally injured on May 13, 1935, while riding his Brough Superior motorcycle (a gift of the G. B. Shaws), a romantic passion for speed having overtaken his former love of exotic adventure. His life passed permanently into myth and literature, as the Robert Bolt film of 1962 and the Terence Rattigan play *Ross* demonstrate, and he provided a character type for many novels written in the thirties and later, such as André Malraux's *The Walnut Trees of Altenburg* (1952).

Although we no longer see him as portrayed in the posed photographs of Lowell Thomas, another figure in the Rudolph Valentino "Sheikh of Araby" texture of the 1920s, his life remains interesting as a true paradigm of the conflicts of romantic men who live into our century. In his role as a character in his own poetic autobiography, he proves one of the first examples in our century of the phenomenon of culture shock, and *Seven Pillars* becomes a glaring and unsettling mirror of his plight.

Our question, however, is not whether Lawrence led an interesting life (he did), but whether or not he produced good literature from it. The literary critic must use Lawrence's life to illuminate his books, and not vice versa. Biographers may share with historians the hard task of sifting documentary evidence; but the literary critic has *Seven*

Pillars and *The Mint* before him. A cool, impartial, and scrupulous literary analysis of both books inevitably leads to the conclusion that Lawrence the artist speaks to us in a voice different and greater than that of Lawrence of Arabia, and certainly much more permanent.

CHAPTER 2

Seven Pillars of Wisdom:
Autobiography and Autobiographies of Travel

I *Autobiography*

BEFORE proceeding any further in our analysis of *Seven Pillars* (and *The Mint*, for that matter), one important and difficult question must be cleared up: what is the genre of Lawrence's books? Is *Seven Pillars* a history of the Arab Revolt, an autobiography, a travel book, a fictionalized autobiography, a confession, a romance-confession, or a memoir? It has been called all these names, and *The Mint* has also been difficult for critics to place precisely.

If we place the *memoir* on one end of the spectrum of auto-biographical writing, labeling it the history of the external events of a life looked at in retrospect by the person who lived that life, and the *confession* on the other end, labeling it the history of the internal events of a life looked at in retrospect by the person who lived that life, then what do we have in the middle? *Autobiography:* the history of the relationship between the external and internal events of a life looked at in retrospect by the person who lived that life. By this definition, both *Seven Pillars* and *The Mint* come off clearly as *autobiographies.* The question remains, what kind?

Until William L. Howarth wrote an excellent article distinguishing the three basic types of autobiography, we had no answer to that question. The first of the three kinds of autobiography Howarth names "Autobiography as Oratory." The foremost example of this kind of autobiography is Henry Adams' *The Education of Henry Adams,* and its characteristics are: (1) it is written to prove a point, and ideology motivates and governs all elements; (2) the narrator sympathizes with the protagonist, but from a great distance, and even uses the third person to name the protagonist, that is, "Adams"; (3) the protagonist relives and learns from his days of sin and error; and (4) a highly shaped rhetorical style of many figures and devices is employed.

Benjamin Franklin's *Autobiography* provides an example of the second type of autobiography, the "Autobiography as Drama." Here we have a narrator who identifies with the protagonist and presents no thesis of character development. The unpretentious and impertinent narrator-protagonist swaggers through picaresque, randomly ordered events changing masks, roles, and identities as he goes along. The shameless writers who fabricate these theatrical autobiographies desire only to portray their own spontaneous minds and characters, rather than to prove a point.

The third type discovered by Howarth, the "Autobiography as Poetry," interests us the most, for Lawrence's work fits clearly into this category, as does Thoreau's *Walden*. Here a narrator who identifies with the protagonist details a tentative, inner journey, making use of the devices of style of the postromantic symbolist poets. Presenting a story of radical dislocation, the poetic autobiographer displays moodiness, unpredictability, identity problems, and a strongly critical image of himself and others. He presents no answers to the many questions about life that he raises, and gives us no clear image of himself: in the end, it is the reader alone who must impose a shape and pattern on the autobiographer's character, who must in fact *create* the autobiographer.[1] As in the case of the other autobiographical types, the personality of the autobiographer is presented in relation to a general framework of historical, social, and personal events.

Seven Pillars of Wisdom (and *The Mint*) can be definitively named an "autobiography as poetry." As such, however, it has one fault, which will be discussed in a later chapter in more detail: Lawrence fails to make clear the precise relationship between inner and outer events. We do not always understand why he is at one moment a friend of the Arabs, at the next disgusted with them, why he is one moment exalted and the next depressed. As a result, the book has a tendency to appear as two halves: a triumphant military plot of romantic adventures, and a bitter personal account of the wounded soul, with no connective tissue. But this fault is less important than it seems. By failing to understand himself and therefore failing to give us a clear picture of the reasons for his spiritual shifts, Lawrence has left his character in *Seven Pillars* open to the reader's imagination. Even more than in most "autobiographies as poetry," the reader must impose his own view to make sense of Lawrence. Both *Seven Pillars* and *The Mint* become, then, truly contemporary reading experiences which would delight the hearts of the theoreticians of the "new novel" and of all critics who believe that the reader must participate in the creation of the story. In form as well as content, Lawrence's autobiographies belong to our age as much as to his. A look at the major influences on Lawrence reveals the extent to which he was original in developing *Seven Pillars'* poetic autobiography.

II *Autobiographies of Travel*

Although Lawrence brings a unique sensibility to bear on his reconstruction of Arabian adventures, *Seven Pillars of Wisdom* represents a variation on and augmentation of a literary tradition of which he was fully aware. The particularly fine haze through which he saw the deserts of Arabia and the people who lived there owes much of its seemingly distinctive tint to the literary treatments of a very select group of writers: authors of the nineteenth-century travel books so popular with the English public, particularly those writers whose travels brought them to the Near East, and W. H. Hudson, the fictional and nonfictional romanticizer of the pampas and wastes of South America.

Despite Lawrence's typical and genuine hero worship and modest self-appraisal, his knowledge of his place in the grand tradition of "Arabian" writers becomes apparent in the following quotation from the foreward he wrote for Bertram Thomas' *Arabia Felix* (1932) in 1932:

> You see, in my day there were real Arabian veterans. Upon each return from the East I would repair to Doughty, a looming giant, white with eighty years, headed and bearded like some renaissance Isaiah. Doughty seemed a past world, in himself; and after him I would visit Wilfred Blunt. An Arab mare drew Blunt's visitors deep within a Sussex wood to his quarried house, stone-flagged and hung with Morris tapestries. There in a great chair he sat, prepared for me like a careless work of art in well-worn Arab robes, his chiselled face framed in silvered, curling hair. Doughty's voice was a caress, his nature sweetness. Blunt was a fire yet flickering over the ashes of old fury.
>
> Such were my Master Arabians, men of forty, fifty years ago. . . .
>
> I suppose no new Sixth Former can help feeling how much his year falls short of the great fellows there when he joined the school. But can the sorry

little crowd of us today be in tradition, even? I fear not. Of course the mere wishing to be an Arabian betrays the roots of a quirk; but our predecessors' was a larger day, in which the seeing Arabia was an end in itself. They just wrote a wander-book and the great peninsula made their prose significant. (Incidentally, the readable Arabian books are all in English, bar one; Jews, Swiss, Irishmen and Whatnots having conspired to help the Englishmen write them. There are some German books of too-sober learning and one Dutch). Its deserts cleaned or enriched Doughty's pen and Palgrave's, Burckhardt's and Blunt's, helped Raunkiaer with his Kuwait, Burton and Wavell in their pilgrimages, and Bury amongst his sun-struck Yemeni hamlets. (xvii-xviii)

Although Lawrence pays homage to almost all his major predecessors, his real admiration remains restricted to those who achieved the finest literary artistry in their travel accounts, as he makes clear in a letter to Sir Percy Sykes written the year after this foreward: "I hope your review, however brief, will recognize the great merit of Palgrave as explorer and writer. . . . He was in the Philby-Thomas class as explorer and wrote brilliantly" (*L*, 768). In this distinction he makes between St. John Philby (the convert to Islam who was the father of Kim Philby, the Communist spy) and Bertram Thomas as great *explorers* and, on the other hand, Palgrave as a great explorer *and* writer, we have the point: Lawrence's reaction to these travel accounts is primarily a literary one. To Robert Graves he writes in 1925 that "E. M. Forster's guide book to Alexandria . . . is great literature, and a good guide. Boost it."[2]

This literary sensitivity to, and judgment of, travel books dates from his earliest letters. On August 2, 1909, during his walking tour of Syria and Palestine, he writes to his mother that the descriptions of the spring at Banias in Eliot Warburton's *The Crescent and The Cross* and Thomson's *The Land and the Book* (both nineteenth-century travel works) are "admirable descriptions" but " 'purple patches,' both of them" (*L*, 70). When in 1910 he describes Hogarth's *A Wandering Scholar in the Levant* (1896) as "one of the best travel books ever written" (*L*, 87), we can safely assume that his criteria for this judgment are primarily literary, a judgment substantiated by my own reading of the book. And the surprising lack of references to Richard Burton's famous *A Pilgrimage to Al-Madinah and Meccah* (1855) in his letters indicates a disapproving literary rather than scientific judgment. A clue to this opinion appears in a letter of 1922, in which Lawrence prefers Lane's translation of the *Arabian Nights* to

Burton's on the basis of style (*L*, 359), although in a letter to Jonathan Cape in the same year, he finds Lane's translation "pompous";[3] and in another letter, he calls Burton's Arabs "pinchbeck."[4]

In the same letter in which he disparages Burton's talent as a translator, Lawrence gives a clear indication of which of his predecessors' books he likes best, as well as the reason for his preference: "*War and Peace* I thought decently written on the whole. Of course not a miracle of style like *Salammbo* or *Moralities Legendaires:* or like Doughty and *Eothen* and *Idle Days in Patagonia*" (*L*, 359). This letter assumes particular importance because it was written while Lawrence was attempting to rewrite the Oxford text of *Seven Pillars*, and not long before or after, as were the other sources quoted. The high value he places on style itself, as well as the rank in which he locates Doughty, Kinglake, and Hudson is obvious. A further indication of Lawrence's literary concern with the travel book shows in a letter he wrote to Cape in 1926 about his own introduction to Doughty's book, *Travels in Arabia Deserta:* "As regards my introduction. *Arabia Deserta*, as a work of art, is better without the discordance of an introduction by a strange hand. Its value doesn't lie in its exactness to life in Arabia (on which I can pose as an authority), but on its goodness as writing."[5]

This quotation provides a clear view into the kind of treatment Lawrence took from the Arabian travel books, particularly Doughty's, which he loved, and applied to *Seven Pillars*. If the travel book is to rely on "goodness as writing" at least as much as on its scientific or "objective" descriptions of peoples, places, and events for its ultimate value, then certain other things about it become obvious.

First, a subjective and in the case of the Anglo-Arabian travel tradition inevitably romanticized account will characterize the author's treatment. Michael Foss explains how and why the Arabian travel book became in the hands of English writers something more than a purely scientific medium:

Those who followed Burton's guide were likely to enter into a world of subtle unreality designed to satisfy a poet's need. . . . Arabia continued to be illumined by the poet's shifting light. For the rest of the nineteenth century, the men who informed England most successfully of that frontier land were poets all—Palgrave, Blunt and Doughty. In the late nineteenth century, an age of scientific rationalism, the rediscovery of Arabia was not a reflection of scientific investigation, but the distorting mirror of the imagination. Perhaps the English public could accept no other presentation; for whereas explorers of unknown countries started with few preconceptions, the Arabian traveller from Europe took with him the historical memories of over a thousand years of conflict with Islam. He necessarily entered into the "fabled" land of the Arabian Nights.[6]

The elements of historical romance and—in the case of the nineteenth-century traveler—Victorian hero worship and a century of Gilbert and Sullivan stylizing in popular media enter the relationship between Englishmen and Arabs at such a deep level that these writers could remain sincerely unconscious of their essentially heightened and unreal view of the desert while transmitting that view to their readers.

At the same moment, the theme of the clash of cultures—the interaction between the personality of the Western traveler and a totally different and for him utterly unassimilable environment and set of mores—comes to provide the main drama or action of these books. While the desire to relive past ages of heroism remains ingrained at the unconscious level, the realities of present discomforts become too intrusive for the traveler to disregard. As a result, Doughty's combination of naturalistic detail and mythologized characters, settings, and dialogue has something in common with Kinglake's blend of Byronic rapture and ironic undercutting. These Arabian travelers *want* to see the heroic and inspiring in the desert from the start, but must constantly come down to earth when they behold the reality. This same combination of unpleasant reality and heroic characters finds its place in *Seven Pillars of Wisdom* as well. But when Jean Beraud-Villars decides that "its balance between romanticism and naturalism was the essence of a new form of literature,"[7] he praises the originality of *Seven Pillars* at some expense to other Arabian travel works in which what the traveler wishes he might have seen and what he actually did see, exist side by side in discordance.

Finally, the individual personalities of the authors, expressed through the medium of powerful and individual styles of writing, come to constitute the most important and striking quality of these works. In Hogarth's phrase, these works are really "autobiographies of travel." (*The Life of Charles M. Doughty*, New York, 1929). The structural cohesion of the travel book relies not on the coherent shaping of incident, but on the sensibility of the author-protagonist. It could scarcely be otherwise when travelers as prone to quirks as our "Arabians" recount long, meandering journeys. Depending on the precise type of "autobiography of travel"—oratorical, dramatic, or poetic, to use Howarth's categories—that they write, the authors become to a certain extent the main characters, and their books guessing-games, with the object for the reader of exploring and shaping the authors' indirectly revealed personalities.

When placed against descriptions and analysis of the works of Kinglake, Doughty, and Hudson—all of which Lawrence read before or during the composition of *Seven Pillars*—Lawrence's use of personal revelations, romantic vision, and an art-prose style becomes an expected and reasonable element of *Seven Pillars,* which still manages to retain its unique individuality of form and content.

A. *Kinglake*

The Near East has long attracted a rare and eccentric kind of Englishman not satisfied with the more mundane interests of Continental grand tours and travel-book writing. As Lawrence wrote, "the mere wishing to be an Arabian betrays the roots of a quirk." Beginning with the establishment of the Levant Company in 1581 and its subsequent explorations in this area, the Near Eastern travel account edged its way from purely commercial interest to the status of an organized, highly self-conscious, and artistic literary genre, which has included among its practitioners such recognized artists as William Thackeray and E. M. Forster.[8]

The publication (1844) of Alexander Kinglake's *Eothen*[9] ("From the East"), a Byronic blend of romantic rapture and undercutting irony, marks the beginning of the artistic period in Anglo-Arabian travel writing. Kinglake's achievement lies in making the writer more important than what he sees in his travels. In the words of Iran Jewett, Kinglake "used the Near East not as an area, but as a literary theme."[10] He transmits his personality through what is obviously a loosely structured, picaresque "autobiography as drama," replete with dramatic scenes and confrontations, and sets the tone of adventurous quest that Lawrence inherits.

What in the end do we learn of Kinglake's character? Although he constantly attacks false romantic pathos, false religious fervor, and viciousness and prejudice in human affairs, he retains quite consciously the religious and political preconceptions of the English traveler of his times. He makes no attempt to meet people of other cultures on their own terms, but always judges them according to standards native to himself. In the end, he clings to a personal, humanistic Christianity, the Greek classics, and British force and moral superiority as Arnoldian "touchstones," however banteringly qualified. Like Doughty and most other nineteenth-century travelers—with the exceptions of the Arabist Burton and the anti-imperialist Blunt—he retains his distance from the alien culture and continues to judge it from on high. He can grant the East only novelty—not moral or cultural equality. Lawrence lacked precisely this certainty, and *Seven Pillars* becomes richer than either *Eothen* or *Arabia Deserta* as a result, whatever the price in personal suffering Lawrence had to pay for his modern, relativistic position. (This point will be investigated more fully in the chapter on the "two veils" of Lawrence's mind). Here, as in his allowing his journey itself to supply the loose structure of his book, Kinglake exerts a negative influence on Lawrence. But in his adventurous view of his travels, his attitude toward Homer, his sometimes guarded use of his personality, and his artistic style, his influence on the later writer can be clearly discerned.

Lawrence rejects Kinglake's imperialism, but he accepts his romanticism. Referring to Lady Hester Stanhope, that amazing figure who is mentioned in Thackeray's *Vanity Fair* and who once faced down a tribe of charging Beduin with a raised umbrella and the single word "Avaunt!" Kinglake remarks that he sees in her (and perhaps, by extension, in himself) "a longing for the East, very commonly felt by proud people when goaded by sorrow." In this tinge of indefinable and inexplicable Byronic pathos, Kinglake touches a chord struck by most Arabian travelers including Lawrence, whose ostensibly inexplicable cause for sorrow at the end of his campaign falls into the category of the common literary effect of the post-Kinglake travel-book writer. And for all Kinglake's spontaneous self-revelation, he tells us that Lady Hester read his character in his face and informed him of the result, but "this, however, I mean to keep hidden." For the most part an open, dramatic autobiographer, Kinglake is not above increasing our interest in his personality by veiling it from us, at least at this point in the book. Like the later Lawrence, Kinglake also understands the value of self-deprecating humor in an autobiography: such expressions as "this poor, pale, solitary self that I always carry around with me" and the "eternal Ego that I am" could not fail to endear him to Lawrence.

Kinglake's romantic love of Homer's *Iliad*—and his dislike of the *Odyssey*—parallels Lawrence's own attitudes toward the Greek poet. We must remember that Lawrence had not yet begun his own *Odyssey* translation until he had already finished reading *Eothen*, and that until he worked on that translation his attitude toward Homer was one of enthusiastic admiration. Perhaps an echo of Kinglake's dislike of the *Odyssey* remained in his mind.

Most of all, Lawrence appreciated *Eothen* for its style. When Kinglake is not indulging in Manfred-like ecstasies, he resorts to biting irony. This use of irony and dramatic technique shields the reader from the horror of Cairo in plague in 1835, just as it keeps the reader from too much romanticism at other points. Kinglake's essential mental health resides in his ability to distance himself through humor from his own foibles and from events. The following passage from the climactic Cairo chapter, a certain "miracle of style," proves an excellent example of his ironic distancing technique; the situation is Kinglake's imaginary view of the thoughts of a European in Cairo dying of plague:

Once more the poor fellow is back home in fair Provence, and sees the sundial that stood in his childhood's garden—sees part of his mother, and the long-since-forgotten face of that dear sister (he sees her, he says, on a Sunday morning, for all the church bells are ringing): he looks up and down through the universe, and owns it well piled with bales upon bales of cotton and cotton eternal—so much so, that he feels—he knows, he swears he could make that winning hazard, if the billiard-table would not slant upwards, and if the cue were a cue worth playing with; but it is not—it's a cue that won't move—his own arm won't move—in short, there's the devil to pay in the brain of the poor Levantine; and perhaps the next night but one he becomes the "life and soul" of some squalling jackal family, who fish him out by the foot from his shallow and sandy grave.

Kinglake's use of dashes and parentheses allow him to create a surrealistic, cinematic effect of partial views, shifting focuses, and wild dreams. As in this chapter in particular and the book as a whole, he moves with ease from one unrelated scene to the next, his eye (and ear) catching every detail of the dying man's frantic associations, and brings us down to a magnificent climax of grim irony. He treats his own bout with the disease with scarcely less irony.

Although Lawrence could never detach himself from his own self or from events as totally as Kinglake, the earlier writer taught him how to combine rapture and irony, romanticism and naturalism, and that fine style in travel writing means the difference between a literary and nonliterary account. However little the tortured and involuted Lawrence has in common with the spontaneous mind of Kinglake, who is able to place such ironic distance between himself and trouble at all times—as Lawrence is not—Kinglake's errors of weak structure and cultural prejudice and his strength as a stylist, an exploiter of his personality, and an honest viewer of desert truths under the romance, could not have been lost on the later writer.

B. *Hudson*

A friend of T. E. and admirer of Doughty, W. H. Hudson practiced the art of the "autobiography of travel" in *Idle Days in Patagonia*[11] as well as that of his more famous novels, *The Purple Land* and *Green Mansions,* to name only a few of his works. Besides the reference to *Idle Days* as a "miracle of style," we have many other signs of Lawrence's pleasure in Hudson's work. On October 4, 1923, he writes to Edward Garnett that

The Hudson's are sumptuous. How well the old man reads in them. *The Shepherd* has found two friendly readers already; yet I like better, much better, the memories of his childhood [in *Far Away and Long Ago*]. Wonderful that one man should have written that and *Patagonia,* and *The Purple Land,* and *Green Mansions:* and I go about thinking that into his first book anyone not a born writer can put all that his spirit holds. Hudson is hardly a born writer, either. Not for him that frenzied aching delight in a pattern of words which happens to run true. (*L,* 433)

By this last somewhat cryptic comment, Lawrence seems to mean that Hudson is a conscious stylist who must work hard to achieve his effects, like Lawrence himself, but that he is no less a fine writer for that. This idea becomes more clear as the letter, one of the most interesting in the Garnett edition, continues:

Do you know that lately I have been finding my deepest satisfaction in the collocation of words so ordinary and plain that they cannot mean anything to a book-jaded mind: and out of some of such I can draw deep stuff. Is it perhaps that certain sequences of vowels or consonants imply more than others: that writing of this sort has music in it? I don't want to affirm it, and yet I would not deny it: for if writing can have sense (and it has: this letter has) and sound why shouldn't it have something of pattern too? My sequences seem to be independent of ear . . . to impose themselves through the eye alone. Do you think that people ever write consciously well? or does that imply an inordinate love for the material, and so ruin the art? I don't see that it should. A sculptor who petted his marbles from sheer joy in their grain and fineness would (pari passu) be better than a mere block-butcher.

So in the end Lawrence dismisses the romantic notion, adhered to by Kinglake who always insists that his pen is not under his control, that style must be an unconsciously directed flow, and believes that a "miracle of style" like *Idle Days* can result from conscious art like his own and Hudson's. A further clarification of his opinion on this point of "conscious" style and on his view of *War and Peace* occurs in a letter of November 6, 1928, to Robert Graves: "A man's a great writer when he can use plain words without baldness. . . . If a fellow isn't big enough he must do the other thing: . . . what you call style:—surface his work. The War-and-Peace plainness is better, perhaps: but one is fonder, often, of the rather less-than-big work. It feels more homelike. That's the reward of secondary writers."[12] Thus, "fine" style, in Lawrence's scheme becomes the tool of the minor writer, in which category he would include himself, since he was such a conscious craftsman. We need not take this misconception about style itself and Lawrence too seriously: it probably arises out of the simple fact that he read Tolstoy in the bland Constance Garnett translation, the only one available in England at that time.

For the most part, Lawrence acts far from apologetic about his enthusiasm for Hudson's work. When Edward Garnett complained of a lack of forthrightness in the "Myself" chapter of *Seven Pillars* and said that "in his books Hudson does not hide his feelings," T. E.'s reply was "Yes! But Hudson is above us all."[13] And as late as 1933, he declares himself "rather saddened" by the lack of "all Hudson, most Conrad, some Doughty" in his Cloud's Hill library (L, 776).

An inadvertent clue to what precisely Lawrence liked in Hudson appears in Richard Haymaker's *From Pampas to Hedgerows and Downs* (New York, 1954). On page 170, Haymaker writes that

The pampas of La Plata, the plains of Patagonia, the countryside of southern England, with their characteristic flora and fauna, are so fully and freshly depicted that they become new realities in the realm of human experience, analogous to the recreation of Selborne, Walden Pond, and the Catskills by White, Thoreau and Burroughs; Dorset and Devon by Hardy, Llewelyn Powys and Williamson; Morocco and the Arabian desert by Loti, Cunning-hame Graham and Doughty. . . .

Haymaker compares Hudson to Doughty, Hardy, Williamson, and Graham, all of whose work Lawrence admired. Specifically, what appealed to Lawrence is Hudson's method of answering a question originally asked by Charles Darwin in his *Voyage of the Beagle* and quoted in *Idle Days* for its appositeness: "Why, then—and the case is not peculiar to myself—have these arid wastes taken so firm possession of my mind?" With Doughty, who found that if "in truth one live with the Aarab, he will have all his life after a feeling of the desert," Hudson can say of the Patagonian desert that "in spite of accurate knowledge, the old charm still exists in all its freshness; and after all the discomforts and sufferings endured in a desert cursed with eternal barrenness, the returned traveller finds in after years that it still keeps its hold on him, that it shines brighter in memory, and is dearer to him than in any other region he may have visited." He heads into the plains of Patagonia drawn by some mysterious force, that common propellant behind most travel books dealing with exotic places: "And yet I had no object in going—no motive which could be put into words; for although I carried a gun, there was nothing to shoot. . . ." Doughty and Lawrence both felt this same mystery, which derives from Kinglake.

Hudson substantiates his love of these plains with a description which undoubtedly moved Lawrence to envy:

> In the scene itself there was nothing to delight the eye. Everywhere through the light, gray mold, gray as ashes and formed by the ashes of myriads of generations of dead trees, where the wind has blown on it, or the rain has washed it away, the underlying yellow sand appeared, and the old ocean-polished pebbles, dull red, and gray, and green, and yellow. On arriving at a hill, I would slowly ride to its summit, and stand there to survey the prospect. On every side it stretched away in great undulations; but the undulations were wild and irregular; the hills were rounded and cone-shaped, they were solitary and in groups and ranges; some sloped gently, others were ridge-like and stretched away in league-long terraces, with other terraces beyond; and all alike were clothed in the gray ever-lasting thorny vegetation. How gray it all was! hardly less so near at hand than on the haze-wrapped horizon, where the hills were dim and the outline blurred by distance.

Hudson appears here as the master romanticizer of landscape, who conjures up a purple land of misty campo, complete with "haze-wrapped horizon," which would no doubt have lured Hemingway's Robert Cohn of *The Sun Also Rises* to expect South America to actually look like that. But Hudson manages this coloring without recourse to the keyed-up metaphors that Lawrence frequently uses. Where Lawrence chooses to focus on the desert's brilliant aspect, Hudson plays this down, relying on balanced phrases and one exclamation mark to create a striking description. By way of contrast with Hudson's fine haze, we remember the heat of Arabia that "came out like a drawn sword and struck us speechless" as Lawrence approaches Jidda. Lawrence must have admired Hudson's ability to accomplish dramatic effects with subtle means.

Similarly, he admired Hudson's easy use of his personality, his lack of reticence in describing and explaining his emotions, his ability to "let go." In a literary use of the memory that precedes Proust's "Madeleine" incident by several years, Hudson in his "Perfume of an Evening Primrose" chapter expands on the meanings that a flower's odor has for him: "The suddenly recovered sensation is more to us for a moment than a mere sensation; it is like a recovery of the irrecoverable past" (p. 244)—*à la Recherchè du temps perdu*. Hudson continues in a Proustian vein when he finds that "I cannot think of any fragrant flower that grows in my distant home without seeing it, so that its beauty may be always enjoyed—but its fragrance, alas, has vanished and returns not!" (p. 244). Just as Lawrence must have studied Hudson's ability to use an "alas!" every now and then and get away with it—an impossible task for a post-romantic modernist writer—so too he must have noted enviously Hudson's ability to emphasize outer rather than inner events in his autobiography, and to be at home with his own personality when he comes to describe it. Although Hudson is a poetic autobiographer who presents life as a search that never ends, and never gives us a concise, clear picture of his personality, which appears only obliquely in *Idle Days*, the amount of ego in the book is sharply controlled by its outer, nature framework. As Robert Hamilton puts it, Hudson "combined insight with interest to a remarkable degree, and his work, though always informed by his unique personality, was objective in intent. He was personal without being an egoist; objective without being shallow."[14] Lawrence may have deplored the lack of structure that *Idle Days* shares with other travel books: it begins with a dramatic opening worthy of the deck of the "Patna" in *Lord Jim*, but Hudson soon diffuses the pressure and the book comes apart as he gets lost on a myriad of subjects. But Hudson's blend of many descriptions of natural scenery and analyses of ideas and an unusually sanguine—for a poetic autobiographer—self that shows itself only through these ideas and descriptions, for the most part, was beyond Lawrence's very self-conscious ability to achieve. By managing to lose himself in objective events, Hudson could afford to be at ease with himself.

Kinglake's totally detached irony, Hudson's emphasis on external events, and—as we shall see—Doughty's stoic reticence could not have influenced a man unsuited by nature to these devices. Lawrence tried making the Arab Revolt more important than himself in *Seven*

Pillars, but failed. Yet Hudson's *Idle Days in Patagonia* provided him with a model, with an author who, in Richard Haymaker's words, "possessed fresh and significant material," and was "a master of a style that could be exquisite, vigorous and eloquent, and a poetic personality."

C. *Doughty*

Lawrence frequently expressed his esteem for Charles Doughty as the greatest of all his predecessors in the Anglo-Arabian travel-book tradition. The introduction he wrote for *Travels in Arabia Deserta* in 1921 offers direct evidence of the depth of his attachment to Doughty's work in the most specific terms, and during the period in which he was engaged in writing and rewriting *Seven Pillars of Wisdom.* For Lawrence, *Arabia Deserta* will remain a monument for its literary artistry no less than for its contribution to the study of the Arabian peninsula:

It is to the outside public willing to read a great prose work, the record of the wanderings of an English poet for two years among the Beduin, that this edition must make its appeal. . . . There is no sentiment, nothing merely picturesque, that most common failing of oriental travel books. . . . It is a book which begins powerfully, written in a style which apparently has neither father nor son, so closely wrought, so tense, so just in its words and phrases, that it demands a hard reader. . . . Mr. Doughty was not content till he had made the book justify the journey as much as the journey justified the book, and in the double power, to go and to write, he will not soon find his rival.

Elsewhere in this introduction, the infusion of Doughty's personality into the book in an indirect manner and the theme of cultural clash figure prominently in the aspects Lawrence singles out for comment, usually to his own self-detriment. Most importantly, Doughty is "never morbid, never introspective," and triumphed over his body to a degree "none of us" did. Doughty refused "to be the hero of his story," also a pointed reference to Lawrence's own case. Finally, Lawrence is "presumptuous" to put his name near "one of the great prose works in our literature."[15]

Although Lawrence remained true to his admiration of Doughty and *Arabia Deserta* all his life, his criticisms of *Arabia Deserta* reveal a sharp analytical eye and indicate not only Doughty's failings, but those common to the travel-book tradition. He made special efforts to

avoid these very faults when it came to writing his own book, but was
not always successful. First, Lawrence realized that he could never
achieve Doughty's stoic reticence and his distancing from himself as
the character Khalil (both traits of the typical "autobiography as
oratory," in Howarth's term) simply because Lawrence's personality
is involuted, self-conscious, and relativistic and totally lacking in the
fixed point of Victorian pride and cultural imperialism. Lawrence
rejected Doughty's simplicity and arrogance of character, as well as
his imperialistic attitude toward the Arabs. Second, in his criticism of
Barker Fairley's standard work on Doughty, Lawrence attacks *Arabia
Deserta*'s lack of artistic structure:

That Barker Fairley book on Doughty spoiled itself, by trying to do too much.
He maintained that the *form* of *A.D.* and *Dawn in Britain* was subtle, and
designed, and balanced, and cumulative. I think it was accident; and a bad
accident. Doughty seems wholly to have lacked the strategic eye which plans
a campaign. . . . *A.D.* is hampered by its lack of form, less only than *Dawn*,
because there was a basis of fact to follow, and life isn't as shapeless as
unassisted and undisciplined art. (*L.*, 526–27)

Lawrence, attempting to become a "master architect" (*S*, 192) of both
war and literature, strives for the kind of comprehensive literary
structure that he felt Doughty was unable to attain. Finally, in a
detailed criticism of Herbert Read's review of *Seven Pillars*,[16] Lawrence, now a member of the R.A.F., elaborates on Doughty's stylistic
faults, sounding less enthusiastic than he had in the 1921 introduction
to *Arabia Deserta:* "These fellows here, with whom I have lived the
last five years, are not so sure in their English as to enjoy *Arabia
Deserta*. Doughty uses hard words for which they would need a
dictionary, and his Scandanavian syntax puzzles them. He closed his
goodness off from the world by not being as honest and simple in
manner as he was in mind" (*L*, 550). In much the same spirit is the
criticism of Doughty's style that he makes in *Men in Print* (1940):
"This inlay of strange words into a groundwork of daily English is a
mistake. The effect is fussy, not primitive, more peasant art than
peasant." On the matters of a too simple view of oneself and one's
surroundings, of weak and digressive structure, and of too precious
style, Lawrence calls Doughty to account. But we should note that
most of Lawrence's criticism of Doughty follows the completion of
Seven Pillars (and Doughty's muted criticism of it),[17] while his
reference to Doughty's book as a "miracle of style" dates from the

years in which he was engaged in continually recasting his own work. Even the most fleeting reference to *Seven Pillars* reveals the extent of Doughty's influence—for both good and evil—on Lawrence.

In the following passage, drawn from the Ibn Rashid court scene in *Arabia Deserta* (which Lawrence especially liked), Doughty's use of archaic style to medievalize and to paint an extremely exotic picture, his use of biblical reference, the projection of his stoic personality, and the clash of cultures theme, are all apparent:

I saluted the Emir, *Salaam aleyk.*—No answer: then I greeted Hamud and Sleyman, now of friendly acquaintance, in the same words, and with *aleykom es salaam* they hailed me smiling comfortably again. One showed me to a place where I should sit down before the Emir, who said shortly "From whence?"—"From my makhzan."—'And what found I there to do all day, ha! and what had I seen in the time of my being at Hayil, was it well?' When the Prince said "Khalil!" I should have responded in their manner *Aunak* or *Labbeyk* or *Tawil el Ummr,* "O Long-of-Age! and what is thy sweet will?" but feeling as an European among these light-tongued Asiatics, and full of mortal weariness, I kept silence. . . . I answered after the pause, "I am lately arrived in this place, but *aghruty,* I suppose it is very well." The Emir opened his great feminine Arab eyes upon me as if he wondered at the not flattering plainness of my speech; and he said. . . . went you in the pilgrimage to the Holy City (Jerusalem)?[18]

The question is, what does Lawrence owe to this art nouveau style and vision, which combines English, Arabic, and sometimes Turkish and Hebrew phrases to form a strange blend which is unlike the English of any period but which does capture the arabesques common to Arabic and its close cousin, Hebrew (in which even today one says "you find favor in my eyes" for "I'm fond of you")?

As much as he attacks Doughty for literary archaism, we frequently find the same linguistic fallacy in Lawrence's book. He literally transposes contemporary Arabic into archaic English, as in his conversation with Tafas: " 'What is upon you, Tafas?' said I" (*S,* 82). On the positive side of stylistic influence, how many of Lawrence's keyed-up descriptions of the desert (such as the passage in which each piece of flint becomes "tipped like a black diamond with flame" [*S,* 607]) owe something to this one sentence of Doughty's?: "The Arabian heaven is burning brass above their heads, and the sand as glowing coals under their weary feet."

Yet Jeffrey Meyers is undoubtedly correct when he writes that "Doughty and Lawrence inevitably have some superficial stylistic similarities—a fondness for Arabic place names, learned references, and lengthy descriptions in ornate and archaic language—but Lawrence's prose is quite different from Doughty's style, which he deliberately rejected as a model for his own book."[19] Doughty's influence was deep, but not on Lawrence's style, at least not directly. The heightened style of Lawrence's dialogues and descriptions reflect the fundamental, chronic lack of ease of its author. For *Seven Pillars*, like *Arabia Deserta*, is a book first and foremost about its author's quest for the absolute in the Arabian desert. We no more accept Doughty's explanation, that his two-year exposure to hardship and danger was the simple fruit of his desire to contribute to geography and the English language, than we ever fully understand the motives behind Lawrence's striving for his unstated and apparently unattainable goal. And the latest biographies of Lawrence— and a recent article on Doughty—despite their claims, fail to define the ultimate motivation of these travelers, a task which the objective observer may well find impossible.[20] As R. P. Blackmur points out, the spirit underlying this famous quotation from *Arabia Deserta* (I, p. 95) remains Doughty's major contribution to Lawrence's view of the desert: "The traveller must be himself, in men's eyes, a man worthy to live under the bent of God's heaven . . . he is such who has a clean human heart and long-suffering under his bare shirt. . . . Here is a dead land, whence, if he die not, he shall bring home a perpetual weariness in his bones. The Semites are like to a man sitting in a cloaca to the eyes and whose brows touch heaven." That Lawrence was cognizant of this quotation appears in his own description of the Arabs as "petty incarnate Semites who attained heights and depths beyond our reach" (S, 586), which simply rephrases the last sentence in the quotation.

Doughty's fundamental romanticizing—while denied by Lawrence—affects him as well. Lawrence's portraits of Auda and Nasir, for instance, owe much to Doughty, whose Sheikh Motlog, "a personable, strong man and well proportioned, of the middle stature, of middle age, and with a comely Jewish visage," who rules his tribe "with a proud humility among the common people" and commands "with a word the unruly Beduw," appears in several reincarnations in *Seven Pillars*. And Lawrence's description of Tallal as "the splendid leader, the fine horseman, the courteous and strong companion of the road" carries in its parallelism the same chivalric ring as Doughty's sentence. But then, "the Asia of Kinglake and Lamartine is wholly gone. . . . and some of us, the medievalists, lament it",

Lawrence had written in 1920,[21] showing how natural this kind of romanticizing was to him.

For the heroic, epic view that Lawrence denied himself in life and in direct statements about his own character in *Seven Pillars* clearly informs that entire book, despite its author. His artistic self allows, like Doughty's, the projection of men larger-than-life set against a stark background of naked desert and searing sun, no matter how many internal debates he presents, no matter how many cynical presentations of the failings of himself and others. He could not feel heroic, grand, at any moment, but through his art we see him and his Arab companions as just that. Thus, as he—like Doughty—can mock men who are "always fond to believe a Romantic tale" (*S*, 562), he can state in a few sentences a contradiction as clear as this: "The epic mode was alien to me, as to my generation. Memory gave me no clue to the heroic, so that I could not feel such men as Auda in myself. He seemed fantastic as the hills of Rumm, old as Malory" (*S*, 549). At the precise moment that his honesty, even in retrospect, will not allow him to see himself as other than small, unheroic, modern as Wilfred Owen, his artistic self's memory of Doughty's medieval treatment of the desert and of Malory's *Morte d'Arthur* and of the fantastic background of the Wadi Rumm, creates a heroic backdrop for understanding the men with whom he worked and whom he consistently and brilliantly led. Despite all Lawrence's—and Doughty's—portrayals of naturalistic hardships and failings, we retain after reading *Seven Pillars* the same essentially "picturesque" view of the desert that Doughty gives us.

Lawrence and Doughty were heroes as disparate as the centuries in which they wrote, the one self-consciously prey to the dragons of a lack of cultural identity and the essential egotism and complexity of the heroic deed, and unable to keep silent about these problems; the other so self-confidently aware of what he achieved and his position in the world that he felt no need to speak openly on the subject. But in the end the two men are artists in the same tradition, that of Kinglake and Hudson as well, and in the end Doughty's literary influence on Lawrence is all-pervasive. For it is Doughty who provided Lawrence with the artistic "clue to the heroic" that he lacked in life and found elsewhere only in the far-removed Homer and Malory, and for which we as readers of *Seven Pillars* must be grateful.

CHAPTER 3

Seven Pillars of Wisdom: *Lawrence as Aesthete and Hero*

DESPITE self-doubts, doubts about his mission, and the knowledge that a true hero in the Homeric sense should not be conscious of his heroism, Lawrence comes across to the reader of *Seven Pillars* as perhaps the last modern hero, the man who successfully achieved his goal in the face of all barriers, internal and external. But Lawrence himself, as the Homer-Achilles of his "introspection epic,"[1] reveals to us the difficulty of waging heroic war in the modern world, clad only in the armor of Homeric ideals and a fin-de-siécle world-weary longing for death. Like Joseph Conrad and Stephen Crane, who straddle the transition from romanticism's last gasp, the "Death in Venice" of a tradition which sees dying bravely as something good, to the new age of Hemingway's antiheroism, Lawrence finds himself facing a new situation with outmoded philosophical tools. The result, as in their cases, is that romantic and antiromantic views of death, among other things, exist side by side in *Seven Pillars* in discordance. Just as we can ask whether or not Lord Jim dies a hero, or if Henry Fleming's encounter with "the great death" has resulted in true heroism or increased self-delusion, so Lawrence as narrator-protagonist combines heroic and antiheroic elements in his vision. When romanticized high ideals clash with bitter modern experience, Lawrence transmutes late Victorian gilt into the jagged shrapnel of the World War I poets and his personal poetry of radical mental fragmentation. From this grating contrast, he forges the powerful if uneven vision that is *Seven Pillars of Wisdom*.

I *Death in Arabia*

As Lawrence lies waiting for the Turks to kill him, having fallen off his charging camel, the lines of Ernest Dowson's "Impenitentia

Ultima" come racing through his head: "For Lord I was free of all Thy flowers, but I chose the world's sad roses,/And that is why my feet are torn and mine eyes are blind with sweat" (S, 304). This memory is entirely appropriate in a book in which death is very frequently reported in the language of late romantic poetry. In this language, death and love are frequently linked, as in the poem in memory of "S.A." which opens *Seven Pillars*: "Love, the way-weary, groped to your body, our brief wage ours for the moment/Before earth's soft hand explored your shape, and the blind worms grew fat upon/Your substance."(S, 5). Ferraj's death becomes a welcome gift in view of the earlier demise of his lover Daud:

We tried to stop the wide, slow bleeding, which made poppy-splashes in the grass; but it seemed impossible, and after a while he told us to let him alone, as he was dying, and happy to die, since he had no care of life. Indeed, for long he had been so, and men very tired and sorry often fell in love with death, with that triumphal weakness coming home after strength has been vanquished in the last battle. (S, 516).

In the chapter on "Strangeness and Pain," the controversial fifth paragraph which deals with Arab homosexual love and appears to have no connection with preceding or following paragraphs, can be explained by this same romantic linkage of death, which is discussed in the third paragraph ("those tired enough to die"), and love. The poetry of death and love or beauty rises to lyrical heights in what is possibly the most famous set piece in the book:

The dead men looked wonderfully beautiful. The night was shining gently down, softening them into new ivory. Turks were white-skinned on their clothed parts, much whiter than the Arabs; and these soldiers had been very young. Close round them lapped the dark wormwood, now heavy with dew, in which the ends of the moonbeams sparkled like sea spray. The corpses seemed flung so pitifully on the ground, huddled anyhow in low heaps. Surely if straightened they would be comfortable at last. So I put them all in order, one by one, very wearied myself, and longing to be of these quiet ones, not of the restless, noisy, aching mob up the valley, quarrelling over the plunder, boasting of their speed and strength to endure God knew how many toils and pains of this sort; with death, whether we won or lost, waiting to end the history. (S, 308)

Lawrence's own longing for death appears here as it does in many other places in *Seven Pillars*.

This longing places Lawrence clearly in the romantic tradition.

Beginning with the Keats of "Ode to a Nightingale," who wishes to merge himself with "easeful Death" and running through the poetry of Tennyson like a bass line, the combination of love and death reaches a height and a climax in the late nineteenth-century cult of death felt clearly in the symphonies of Gustav Mahler. H. Rider Haggard's *She*, which traces a journey through a dead land, burial caves, and the veil of life itself, and Conrad's *Heart of Darkness* with its imaginative anthropology of a voyage into unknown darkness, are both Mahlerian death "trips," in whose Ayesha and Kurtz are also seen the late romantic vision of Faustian supermen. Both stories inevitably involve love as well—Ayesha's for Kallicrates, Kurtz' sweetheart's for him. In an excellent essay on Lawrence and Nietzsche, Jeffrey Meyers has traced the element of the will in *Seven Pillars;* Thomas J. O'Donnell has brilliantly discussed Lawrence as late nineteenth-century artistic rebel,[2] which can be related to Kurtz' and Ayesha's breaking of bounds; but the significance of Lawrence's flirtation with death remains to be explained. First, let us look at the more superficial level.

"The Sword Also Means Cleanness and Death" proclaims the motto on *Seven Pillars'* front cover, and of course we expect writing about death in a war story. But in fact Lawrence is a late nineteenth-century aesthete, one of "the last Romantics" in Yeats' phrase, and war only provides him with an opportunity for shaping death in the image of that philosophy. On the level of literary influence, Lawrence simply adopts the style and mannerisms that he learned from his favorite writers. Who exactly (in addition to the travel writers) were these? This is important to establish in view of Lawrence's many admissions of literary borrowing, one of which appears in a letter to William Rothenstein: "My style is a made-up thing, very thickly encrusted with what seemed to me the tit-bits and wheezes of established authors. . . . There isn't any good, any permanence, in such a derivative effort."[3] Lawrence's borrowings, which in fact add to the rich resonance of his styles despite his disclaimer, derive from classical Latin and Greek authors as well as medieval chroniclers and modern French and English writers. But although the abstruse Bernardino Telesio ("Telesius") and Syrian Greek poets, among others, add an exotic touch to reading which also included the more commonplace Rudyard Kipling and Henry Williamson, in fact the books Lawrence most enjoyed offer few surprises in terms of his period as an undergraduate.

Vyvyan Richards provides the best reconstruction of his friend's taste in literature. In the picture he paints in his excellent *Portrait of T. E. Lawrence* (1936), late Victorians take precedence, with a lesser emphasis on early twentieth-century writers. He stresses the importance of the Morris cult in vogue while he and Lawrence were at Oxford, and its carry-over into Lawrence's later life. Even Lawrence's antiquarian eccentricities fit into the perfect catalog of Oxford Edwardian tastes that Lawrence's reading constitutes. What is surprising is that these authors remained his favorites throughout his life, with few changes.

Thus, Richards mentions specifically Christina Rossetti's "The Martyr," Tennyson's "Palace of Art" and "Dream of Fair Women," Rolfe's "Don Tarquino" ("favoured especially for its 'fleshliness' "), "Gods and Their Makers" by Housman, and "most of Walter Pater." Aeschylus, a required part of the great Oxford classics course which trained many empire builders, Shakespeare, and Shelley complete this early picture, with Nietzsche, Frank Dobson, William Roberts, Robert Graves, and James Joyce entering later. "Rupert Brooke he compared with Keats for his techniques; but found him much too restrained to be as musical as Keats could be. He admired W. H. Hudson and had most of his writings." Above all, "Morris, Doughty, Aristophanes and Malory went with him from boyhood to his death" (pp. 29-30).

Lawrence's love of the late romantics and censure of antiromantics appears as late as 1938, in a letter to David Garnett: "Really, people are odd. They are writing apologetically of Rossetti, in the papers, everywhere. He was a magnificent poet. Morris is half-praised. Morris was a giant. Somebody said Dowson wasn't a great poet; or Flecker. God Almighty! Must everyone be as seven-leagued as Milton and Byron and Hardy?" (*L,* 612). In a list of preferred reading compiled well after the writing of *Seven Pillars,* he lists Morris as his favorite writer.[4]

During the Arabian campaign itself, Lawrence's reading matter consisted of " . . . the *Morte:* Aristophanes (I read all the *Peace,* very gratefully, & without much technical trouble) and *The Oxford Book of English Verse. . ."* (*L,* 512). Besides Lawrence's 1835 Dinsdorf edition of Aristophanes in the original Greek, the Houghton Library at Harvard holds the 1915 edition of *The Oxford Book of English Verse* which Lawrence "Bought in Cairo 1916. Carried through Hejaz and Syria 1917–1918" according to the note above his initials on the flyleaf. Graves writes about this book that its influence "on his feelings and actions during the campaign would be well worth studying. The copy survives with marginal annotations, many of these dated."

The poems in the index of first lines of this vellum-bound book have been marked in pencil with from one to four dashes, which confirm Lawrence's romantic tastes, which include the Cavalier poets and Burns and exclude all neoclassical poets except Gray. Lawrence's choice of poems for his own private anthology, *Minorities*, edited in 1971 by J. M. Wilson[5] but originally envisaged as a supplement to the *Oxford Book,* simply supplements the picture already outlined.

The result of this reading, so different from the tastes of a post World War I modernist, were noted by Lawrence himself: "It's odd, you know, to be reading these [Eliot's] poems, so full of the future, so far ahead of our time; and then to turn back to my book, whose prose stinks of coffins and ancestors and armorial hatchments. Yet people have the nerve to tell me it's a good book! It would have been, if written a hundred years ago: but to bring it out after *Ulysses* is an insult to modern letters. . ." (*L*, 488). When we find the captured Turkish musicians in *Seven Pillars* referred to as a "pale crew of bearded, emaciated men with woe-begone faces" (*S*, 74), we catch an unmistakable echo of Keats' "La Belle Dame Sans Merci," which Lawrence includes in *Minorities.* But in addition to hundreds of such allusions in phrases, Lawrence's favorite reading results in "aesthetic" description, medievalizing of characters in the manner of Rossetti and the Pre-Raphaelites, and of course the black romance of death and homosexual love already noted. We find everywhere that "exquisite" sensitivity to color that is a pose of the 1890s: "It was pretty to look at the neat, brown men in the sunlit sandy valley, with the turquoise pool of salt water in the midst to set off the crimson banners which two standard bearers carried in the van" (*S*, 163). Huysmans' Des Esseintes (and Lawrence read *A Rebours* in 1922) or Wilde's Dorian Gray could have spoken the following: "As we went, the brushwood grouped itself into thickets whose massed leaves took on a stronger tint of green the purer for their contrasted setting in plots of open sand of a cheerful delicate pink" (*S*, 351). Here his self-consciousness qualifies full "aesthetic" indulgence: "Fellows were very proud of being in my bodyguard, which developed a professionalism almost flamboyant. They dressed like a bed of tulips, in every colour but white; for that was my constant wear, and they did not wish to presume" (*S*, 465).

Lawrence, as Oxford aesthete, finds himself in a situation almost too good to be true: the leader of a rebellion against established authority amid an exotic people remote from all "civilization." Of course we find his abnormally, deliberately oversensitive, heightened sense of color contributing brightness to a chivalric, medieval blend of characters who owe more to Morris, Doughty, Malory, and Homer than to any "objective" vision. Just as Vyvyan Richards claims that the "long beduin tents reminded Lawrence of the Scandanavian halls of the Morris sagas," so A. W. Lawrence finds among the Arabs "a spirit that would appeal to such a lover of the *Morte D'Arthur*."[6] Feisal first appears like a noble Saladin out of the Richard Coeur-de-Lion stories, looking "very tall and pillar-like, very slender, in his long white silk robes and his brown head-cloth bound with a brilliant scarlet and gold cord. His eyelids were dropped; and his black beard and colourless face were like a mask against the strange, still watchfulness of his body. His hands were crossed in front of him on his dagger" (*S*, 91). The march on Owais (which appears in almost the same form in the *Arab Bulletin,* the main differences being the use of "purple" for "faded crimson" and "gold" for "gilt")[7] in its chivalric tone seems to combine equal doses of Malory, Doughty, Morris, Huysmans, as well as cool Oxfordisms:

The march became rather splendid and barbaric. First rode Feisal in white, then Sharraf at his right in red head-cloth and henna-dyed tunic and cloak, myself on his left in white and scarlet, behind us three banners of faded crimson silk with gilt spikes, behind them the drummers playing a march, and behind them again the wild mass of twelve hundred bouncing camels of the bodyguard, packed as closely as they could move, the men in every variety of colured clothes and the camels nearly as brilliant in their trappings. We filled the valley to its banks with our flashing stream. (*S*, 140–41)

Lawrence constantly uses the words "chivalric" and "heroic," and although he refers to himself at one point as a "theatre knight" and thus undercuts his brilliant backdrop with personal ironies—much in the manner of Kinglake, who is always willing to go from the subline to the ridiculous—his main characters remain epic, larger-than-life in our minds. Auda, for instance, enters like a "knight-errant" of the desert, and "saw life as a saga. All the events in it were significant: all personages in contact with the heroic. His mind was stored with poems of old raids and epic tales of fights, and he overflowed with them on the nearest listener" (*S*, 223). As T. E. himself put it on the last page of the 1922 Oxford text of *Seven Pillars,* "The Arabs made a chivalrous appeal to my young instinct. . . ."

Although Lawrence translated the *Odyssey* long after he completed *Seven Pillars,* Homer's vision plays a major role in the character of Lawrence as we see him in his book, and influences the view that Lawrence as author takes of his characters. In the words of James A. Notopoulos, Lawrence's "splendor as a human being and a writer cannot be understood without the metaphors of the *Odyssey* and the *Iliad.* Both of these poems enter into his experiences, his writing, and into shaping his outlook. Homer was a lifelong study with Lawrence and he emerges as one of his finest translators. That he read him as part of his schooling in England is taken for granted. Homer followed him to the dig of Carcemish by the Euphrates. . . . He discusses the *Iliad* with Thomas Hardy for whom Homer was also a companion. Homer follows him to Karachi where he spent all his off-duty hours in translating the *Odyssey.*"[8]

As Notopoulos points out, "The Arab had the very characteristics of Homer's warriors: individualism, family pride in the heroic code of honor, revenge, joy in arms, in booty, and as Lawrence observed, 'to an Arab an essential part of the triumph was to wear the clothes of an enemy.' " (p. 340). Not only did the Arabs offer Lawrence "a theme ready and epic" (*S*, 549) for Homeric glorification in literature, but as Avraham Feinglass has pointed out,[9] Lawrence's reading of Homer actually allowed him to act out the role of the primitive hero whom the Beduin would respect. Lawrence mentions the "Beersheba Beduin" (*S*, 484). I interviewed two older members of the tribe settled at Tel Sheva, just a few miles outside of modern Beersheba, to find out if they knew anything of Lawrence. One answered immediately, "Sure—I've seen the movie!" and the second claimed that she had heard stories that Lawrence had slept in her father's tent, a tale equivalent to a Near Eastern "Washington Slept Here" declaration. Feinglass, a member of a kibbutz in the Beersheba area, had only slightly better luck. Although he learned nothing directly of Lawrence, he turned to Elihu Nawi, the present mayor of Beersheba and the compiler of an anthology of folk tales, *Stories of the Arabs* (1972), who recommended to him Aref el-Aref's *Bedouin Love, Law and Legend* (1944) as a source of factual information about Beduin customs. According to Feinglass, the book's author "was for many years the District Officer of Beer Sheva under the British Mandate Government." Further, according to Achsein Suleiman el Asad, a Beduin of the el Asad Tribe in Beersheba District, whom Feinglass interviewed, Aref el-Aref is remembered by the

Beduin as the "first man in history to be able to successfully conduct a census among the Bedouin."[10]

Aref el-Aref's comments on the Beduin way of life, quoted by Feinglass, prove that Lawrence had some solid basis for his view of the Beduin as Homeric heroes who in his time still lived according to a very harsh code which he practiced with difficulty: "When the Badawi complains it may be accepted readily that he has a very real cause and that he has suffered beyond bearing. He is a patient soul, almost stoic in his forebearance. He will face extremes of heat and cold without a murmur, go for two days without food or drink should the need arise, and undergo great feats of physical endurance to complete a task or keep a promise."[11] To confirm this and Lawrence's (and Doughty's) view of the harshness of Beduin ways, Feinglass quotes the sociologist Emanuel Marx, who "As late as 1967 . . . described the Bedouin diet as more than enough to lessen the enthusiasm of the average Westerner choosing to live among them."[12] Lawrence is not remembered by the Beduin of the Beersheba area whom Feinglass and I have interviewed because his major contact with Beduin was restricted to the tribes farther east, among them the Beni Sakhr and Howeitat, who even today form the backbone of King Hussein's Jordan Arab Legion. But when he describes them as tough warriors and superimposes on them Homeric phrases, and speaks of his own difficulty in imitating their mores, we can now understand why. Like Auda and like the Beersheba Beduin to whom I have talked, we may well believe that, at least in terms of physical endurance, "The world is greater as we go back."

Notopoulos notes apropos of Lawrence's *Odyssey* the interesting fact that "As one who had lived with Arab oral bards, to such an extent that he even made an amusing parody of the formulaic style in a story to paraody Auda's incorrigible epic addiction, Lawrence failed to perceive the oral style of the *Odyssey*" (p. 339). But in writing *Seven Pillars*, Lawrence remembered well the epic vision that the desert had allowed him to glimpse, the old heroism that could laugh at death. As Notopoulos points out, "Lawrence's chief fascination with Auda, however, was the warrior's delight in war and the delirium of the brave. The crescendo of the epic action of the book coincides with Auda's exhibition of the delirium of the brave. . . . Lawrence's description of Auda's furious charge at Aba el Lissan . . . is sheer Homeric."

Lawrence himself undergoes the stages necessary to the creation of all heroes: separation (his lone mission among the Arabs); initiation (his tutelage in Arab ways under Feisal); confrontation (his touching "the great death," in Stephen Crane's words, in battle); and return to society, after having paid for and exorcised its sins like Christ (this return occurs only in Part 3 of *The Mint*). But, as we shall see, his dual role as Homer and Achilles caused problems unknown to Homer himself, who wrote fiction and not autobiography. In any case, both his late romanticism and the Homeric tradition, in which death and homosexual love are also linked (as in the death of Achilles' lover Patroclus in the *Iliad*), unite to produce, on the superficial, literary level, Lawrence's fin-de-siècle treatment of death in *Seven Pillars.*

However, the real reason for Lawrence's linkage of love and death throughout *Seven Pillars* finds no direct expression there or in any other source: according to Tom Beaumont, a British machine gunner who served with Lawrence, it was during September, 1918, at Umtaiye that Lawrence told him of the death of Salim Achmed, "S. A.," or Dahoum, Lawrence's Arab servant. [13] At the very moment that the campaign was reaching its victorious conclusion, Salim Achmed, whom Lawrence employed as a spy behind enemy lines, was dying of typhoid. When we make the connection between "S. A." and Salim Achmed, the tactile feeling of the "S. A." poem becomes important: "Love, the way-weary, groped to your body, our brief wage/ours for the moment/Before earth's soft hand explored your shape, and the blind/worms grew fat upon/Your substance." Although Lawrence remained all his life a puritan who called physical love of both the heterosexual and homosexual varieties "beastly" and stated at least twice that he had never had voluntary sexual experience, [14] as well as the fact that "The disgust of being touched revolted me more than the thought of death and defeat . . ." (S, 532), it seems obvious that Lawrence learned through Dahoum if not full sexuality then at least to allow himself to be touched. By Part 3 of *The Mint* Lawrence can touch and be touched; he is able to achieve there the reorientation of the senses toward the tactile East that Whitman advocates in *Leaves of Grass*, one of Lawrence's favorite books (*L*, 467). No one can say with certainty that Lawrence was a practicing, overt homosexual, but his sympathetic treatment of Ferraj and Daud and other male Arab lovers, and this connection with S. A., indicate that at the least he longed for a breaking down of the prison walls of puritanical restrictions on sensuality and a puritanical over-conscientiousness and possibly experienced this himself to some degree.[15] Most likely, his relationship with Dahoum was idealized and included some limited excursion into the sense of touch, but nothing more. This remains speculative, but what is clear is that Lawrence links death, love, and heroism in many parts of *Seven Pillars* because death, the heroic frenzy, or delirium, and the love he experienced with Dahoum, all contribute to the loss of self-consciousness and to the opening of the self to the world spirit. For Lawrence, the merging of the self with the universe remains the ultimate, absolute goal.

II *The Other Side of the Coin*

If *Seven Pillars* offers a romantic view of death, love, and heroism, it also presents antiheroic scenes and opinions worthy of Wilfred Owen and Hemingway. In 1934, Lawrence wrote to a young writer that "The very young often are half in love with Death—and half afraid of him. Later, when Death is nearer, you will be reluctant to think so closely of him."[16] In fact, the close reader of *Seven Pillars* detects clearly the harsh and repulsive reality under the romantic veil. Lawrence dreamed of a world of heroic glory which he glimpsed sometimes among the Beduin; but as a modern man and despite the force of his will to push his body to the breaking point, he suffers the fate of the sensitive intellectual forced to participate in brutal and bloody deeds and almost breaks down as a result. As James Notopoulos correctly writes, "He exhibits the dilemma of a modern figure who experienced the Homeric delirium of the brave and wrote of it with the requisite magic of literature, yet was condemned to tragic frustration by the anachronism of the heroic act in our times. . . . Lawrence could not write the simple direct kind of epic. It had to be an epic fashioned out of complex factors."

Some of these factors are (1) the knowledge that he is working for Britain as well as the Arabs, and is therefore not the true leader of a national liberation movement that he would like to be; (2) constant self-consciousness of the role of "hero" who must imitate and parody Auda rather than experience the simple directness of Auda's emotions; and (3) a repulsion from brutality and cruelty and a too hard physical and mental test.

Throughout *Seven Pillars*, Lawrence makes no attempt to hide the reality of the revolt under the glory:

The mud roof dripped water all the day long, and the fleas on the stone floor sang together nightly, for praise of the new meats given them. We were twenty-eight in the two tiny rooms, which reeked with the sour smell of our crowd.

In my saddle-bags was a *Morte d'Arthur*. It relieved my disgust. The men had only physical resources; and in the confined misery their tempers roughened. Their oddnesses, which ordinary time packed with a saving film of distance, now jostled me angrily; while a grazed wound in my hip had frozen, and irritated me with painful throbbing. Day by day, the tension among us grew, as our state became more sordid, more animal. (*S*, 485–86)

Lawrence escapes into romance as a character; as author, he reveals both reality and escape, both the sordid conditions and his reading of the *Morte d'Arthur*. When one of his men must be whipped for an infraction of discipline, Lawrence feels "sorry for Awad; his hardness put me to shame" (*S*, 486). Beduin life was indeed hard, and however many allusions it caused to spring into the mind of a romantic temperament, we feel a revulsion lurking under the Homeric glory:

> The valley was a weird sight. The Arabs, gone raving mad, were rushing about at top speed bareheaded and half-naked, screaming, shooting into the air, clawing one another nail and fist, while they burst open trucks and staggered back and forward with immense bales, which they ripped by the rail-side, and tossed through, smashing what they did not want. . . . To one side stood thirty or forty hysterical women, unveiled, tearing their clothes and hair; shrieking themselves distracted. The Arabs without regard to them went on wrecking the household goods; looting their absolute fill. . . .
>
> Seeing me tolerably unemployed, the women rushed, and caught at me with howls for mercy. I assured them that all was going well: but they would not get away till some husbands delivered me. These knocked their wives off and seized my feet in a very agony of terror of instant death. A Turk so broken down was a nasty spectacle: I kicked them off as well as I could with bare feet, and finally broke free. (*S*, 369)

Primitive epics certainly contain rushes for spoils and occasionally a cowardice that is despised, but they are narrated by primitive poets contemporary with these events. The irony with which Lawrence narrates this episode ("I assured them that all was going well"; "till some husbands delivered me") indicates that the whole scene appears sordid to him, however Homeric it might be. Lawrence's life as leader of a "Homeric" band certainly was not easy, either with the men or with other leaders: in Chapter 90, Lawrence reports Zeid's irresponsible squandering of the gold necessary for further action, which "meant the complete ruin of my plans and hopes, the collapse of our effort to keep faith with Allenby" (*S*, 500) and results in

Lawrence's only attempt to quit the revolt altogether; and even Feisal "showed himself hot-tempered and sensitive, even unreasonable, and he ran off soon on tangents" very early in the adventure (S, 97).

As difficult as it was for a modern, highly educated Englishman to witness such events as the hunting of defeated men ("The Arabs on their track rose against them and shot them ignobly as they ran" [S, 482]), even brutal enemies, it was much more difficult when the detached viewing gave way to involvement, participation:

> I made him enter a narrow gully of the spur, a dank twilight place overgrown with weeds. Its sandy bed had been pitted by trickles of water down the cliffs in the late rain. At the end it shrank to a crack a few inches wide. The walls were vertical. I stood in the entrance and gave him a few moments' delay which he spent crying on the ground. Then I made him rise and shot him through the chest. He fell down on the weeds shrieking, with the blood coming out in spurts over his clothes, and jerked about till he rolled nearly to where I was. I fired again, but was shaking so that I only broke his wrist. He went on calling out, less loudly, now lying on his back with his feet towards me, and I leant forward and shot him for the last time in the thick of his neck under the jaw. His body shivered a little, and I called the Ageyl; who buried him in the gully where he was. Afterwards the wakeful night dragged over me, till, hours before dawn, I had the men up and made them load, in my longing to be free of Wadi Kitan. They had to lift me into the saddle. (S, 181–82)

Lawrence's hand shakes, and the act of killing makes him physically and morally sick. Instead of the poetry of death and oversensitive painting of colors that typifies Ferraj's brave death, here we have only the stark reportage of horror. Neither Auda's nor Odysseus' hands would have shook. When Lawrence deals with brave and noble death, or with justified revenge killing (as of the Turks at Deraa for their torture of him a year earlier and their brutality toward the villagers of Tafas, in Chapter 117), he assumes the Homeric tone; but in an instance like the above, he can find no flicker of grandeur, and his soft modernity betrays the epic pose. In the course of the revolt, Lawrence had to do—and witness—many deeds that could never be called heroic.

For this and other reasons, Lawrence had great difficulty in seeing himself as a hero, as he tells us in Chapters 99 and 100. Written in a difficult, opaque prose—to which Lawrence always resorts when describing his thoughts—these chapters actually contain an honest and brilliant, if sometimes confused, statement on modern heroism (or antiheroism) that repays close reading. In them, we find that Lawrence is a Homer who sees some old-time heroes like Auda and Tallal but who cannot himself participate in their mentality. While Auda fights for the cause of Arab freedom, Lawrence only parodies him as he parodies his epic style of oral poetry in Chapter 48. In fact, Lawrence feels that he is a British agent, sent to live "my outcast life among these Arabs, while I exploited their highest ideals and made their love of freedom one more tool to help England win" (S, 544). As such, "the stranger, the godless fraud inspiring an alien nationality" (S, 548), Lawrence feels that he did too good a job: as he tells us in Chapter 1, a man following his model among the Arabs "may imitate them so well that they spuriously imitate him back again" (S, 31). Thus any heroism Lawrence may display is only an act and a tool of the British government, which he felt betrayed promises of independence that he made to the Arabs: "If I did not hesitate to risk my life, why fuss to dirty it? Yet life and honour seemed in different categories, not able to be sold one for another: and for honour, had I not lost that a year ago when I assured the Arabs that England kept her plighted word?" (S, 545). But in fact the problem of heroism that Lawrence raises goes far beyond one specific case of dual loyalties:

With man-instinctive, anything believed by two or three had a miraculous sanction to which individual ease and life might honestly be sacrificed. To man-rational, wars of nationality were as much a cheat as religious wars, and nothing was worth fighting for: nor could fighting, the act of fighting, hold any meed of intrinsic virtue. Life was so deliberately private that no circumstances could justify one man in laying violent hands upon another's: though a man's own death was his last free will, a saving grace and measure of intolerable pain. (S, 548)

When watching Auda or imitating very well and deeply the Arabs' fervor, Lawrence could be "man-instinctive"; but in "man-rational" the Hemingway note of total disillusionment enters. "Among the Arabs I was the disillusioned, the sceptic, who envied their cheap belief" (S, 549). Lawrence would like to believe fully in the idea of a national war, but simply cannot.

Now Lawrence discusses the rationalizations which he practiced on himself in order to get through the revolt, and dismisses them; the most enticing of these is the idea that "our endurance might win redemption, perhaps for all a race" (S, 550). Instead of simply accepting this possibility, Lawrence admits the truth of the matter:

Yet in reality we had borne the vicarious for our own sakes, or at least because it was pointed for our benefit: and could escape from this knowledge only by a make-belief in sense as well as motive.

The self-immolated victim took for his own the rare gift of sacrifice; and no pride and few pleasures in the world were so joyful, so rich as this choosing voluntarily another's evil to perfect the self. There was a hidden selfishness in it, as in all perfections. To each opportunity there could be only one vicar, and the snatching of it robbed the fellows of their due hurt. . . .

To endure for another in simplicity gave a sense of greatness. There was nothing loftier than a cross, from which to comtemplate the world. The pride and exhilaration of it were beyond conceit. (S, 550–51)

In other words, it would be nice to ascribe glorious motives to one's actions, even the sacrificing of one's honor; but in the end one has to admit that all sacrifices are selfish. Ideally an Arab should have led this revolt, and Lawrence feels that he is indulging his need for adulation by taking the place of a real Arab leader.

Most of all, "Honest redemption must have been free and child-minded. When the expiator was conscious of the under-motives and the after-glory of his act, both were wasted on him" (S, 551). As a "modern man" who is "thought-riddled" (S, 551), Lawrence must analyze the heroic act, instead of simply accepting it. Once the act is analyzed, the magic is gone. With such an overactive conscience and analytical faculty, Lawrence had to feel that "There seemed no straight walking for us leaders in this crooked lane of conduct, ring after ring of unknown, shamefaced motives cancelling or double-charging their precedents" (S, 551–52).

As the revolt continues, Lawrence's involvement in it grows, and so does his self-consciousness and guilt, although these are never fully explained to us:

I had had no concern with the Arab Revolt in the beginning. In the end I was responsible for its being an embarrassment to its inventors. Where exactly in the interim my guilt passed from accessory to principal, upon what headings I should be condemned, were not for me to say. Suffice it that since the march to Akaba I bitterly repented my entanglement in the movement, with a bitterness sufficient to corrode my inactive hours, but insufficient to make me cut myself clear of it. Hence the wobbling of my will, and endless, vapid complainings. (S, 552)

Lawrence's personal eccentricities have been stressed by biographers and critics as reasons for his feelings; but in these two chapters he has said things which Crane and Hemingway and Conrad have also said: he has explained why it is hard to be a hero in the modern world. When he thinks that "Death in the air would be a clean escape" (S, 545) from the guilt of a man who cannot rationalize his actions, no matter how heroic they seem to the crowd, he speaks beyond all romantic poses as a man truly sick of life. If in the end we take away with us a heroic view of Lawrence as one who succeeded despite all difficulties in getting to Damascus, we do so despite Lawrence's own view of himself.

If we look at the portrayal of love and death through Lawrence's realistic rather than romantic veil, we find a totally contradictory view of these things that causes a discordance throughout the book. In the realistic view, death is presented as the last resort of a man pressed too far, or a brutal, savage, and meaningless event caused by the primitive instincts aroused by war. When practiced by the Bey at Deraa, who uses compulsion rather than the free choice offered by the Arabs, homosexual love becomes anything but beautiful or heroic, an involuntary, violent, and destructive assault on the citadel of self. War and the arbitrary power afforded by war become excuses for the rape of the integrity of the individual and of civilized feeling itself.

Lawrence fuses the reality and the romance wonderfully in the symbolism of the Turkish barracks of Chapter 121. As Lawrence enters, he meets the "sickening stench" and "sight" (S, 656) of rotting and dying bodies which have been totally neglected. This is the underside of glory, the dirt swept under the rug of war. "I picked forward a little between their lines, holding my white skirts about me, not to dip my bare feet in their puddled running . . ." (S, 656). The white purity of the heroic ideal can barely escape the contamination of reality. When a medical major slaps Lawrence in the face for brutishness, we share Lawrence's sense that he to some degree deserved this treatment, for "anyone who pushed through to success a rebellion of the weak against their masters must come out of it so stained in estimation that afterward nothing in the world would make him feel clean" (S, 659). If we see Lawrence as a hero at the end, we also know the price such heroism exacts in the modern world. Lawrence writes as a Homer whose *Iliad* has absorbed into it the bitterness of Shakespeare's *Troilus and Cressida,* or Hemingway's *The Sun Also Rises.* Do we cynically mock his Achilles as a man who should have known better, or weep over the tragedy of a man who had to learn too much?

CHAPTER 4

Seven Pillars of Wisdom: *Dramatized Truth in Autobiography*

I *Texts of* Seven Pillars

IN *Abinger Harvest*, E. M. Forster comments with antischolarly irony that the profusion of variant manuscripts has made *Seven Pillars* a "joy" for students of the book.[1] Judging from the number of conflicting views surrounding these different manuscripts, he could have used the word "sorrow" with equal justice, although some scholars have gotten many articles out of exploiting and in my opinion exaggerating the importance of the variations in these manuscripts. In any case, the story of the composition and revision of *Seven Pillars* has been told thoroughly by Thomas O'Donnell and Jeffrey Meyers.[2] My purpose now is simply to label the texts for the reader's convenience: (1) Text I: Begun January 10, 1919, in Paris and finished July 25, 1919. The whole text, except for the introduction, was lost at Reading Station, November, 1919. (2) Text II: Begun December 2, 1919, at Oxford and then dropped until January–February, 1920, when ninety-five percent was written at Barton Street in thirty days. Finished May 11, 1920, at Barton Street and corrected and added to slowly for nearly two years. Destroyed by Lawrence May 10, 1922, except for one single specimen page which is inserted after the Epilogue of Text III. (3) Text III: This is the Bodleian manuscript. Begun September 1, 1920, and finished May 9, 1922, at 14 Barton Street, with parts written in Jedda and Amman. (4) Text IV: The Oxford text. This is Text III printed up in eight copies on the press of the Oxford *Times* from January 20, 1922, to June 24, 1922. I have examined the copy of this text at the Houghton Library at Harvard. Except for front and end matter, it is the same as the Bodleian manuscript essentially but the length of both texts (330,000 words)

makes it very difficult to compare more than selected passages.
(5) The Subscriber's Edition of 1926: This is what I refer to as the "final
edition" and is the same as the Dell, Garden City, and Penguin
editions except for very minor details. The Penguin edition, not
available in America, contains an introductory chapter of the Subscriber's Edition absent from American editions. The Subscriber's
Edition was distributed to a select group of either 211 or 217 persons.[3]
It is 280,000 words long. (6) *Revolt in the Desert* (1927): This is an
abridged, 130,000-word version of *Seven Pillars* issued for popular
consumption and amounts to a memoir rather than an autobiography
because all personal, introspective passages have been eliminated.

Actually, the manuscript history of *Seven Pillars* is even more
detailed and complicated than appears here, but this outline will do
for our purposes. When we discuss Lawrence's different self-
portraits, we will be discussing variations between Text III (the
Bodleian manuscript) and Text IV (the Oxford text) on the one hand,
and the final edition, in my case that put out by the Garden City
Publishing Co. and identical with the 1926 edition, on the other.

In the course of his many revisions, Lawrence published material
from his manuscripts in article form in various journals. Some of these
have been made available by Stanley and Rodelle Weintraub, under
the title *Evolution of a Revolt* (1967). And as noted in my last chapter,
we have in *Secret Despatches from Arabia* the intelligence reports
that Lawrence sent to his superiors in the Arab Bureau in Cairo
during the revolt, and which were originally published in the
Bureau's secret *Arab Bulletin* newsletter for intelligence purposes.

II *Dramatized Truth*

One very important factor that distinguishes autobiography from
fiction is the expectation of literal factual and historical truth that the
reader of an autobiography brings to his text. He wants to feel that the
writer actually experienced both the inner and outer events that he
narrates, and if it transpires that the writer has invented some or all of
these events, the reader feels duped. Yet anyone who has studied the
genre of autobiography knows that a certain tension inevitably exists
between the bare, factual, chronological internal and external events
of a life, and the stylistic, temporal, spatial, and ideological form in
which they are expressed in the autobiography itself. In the various
acts of remembering, selecting, arranging, and basically making
readable the raw material of his life, or a portion of his life, the
autobiographer puts together a self-portrait which, like a painted

self-portrait,[4] may closely resemble or differ greatly from a mirror image. In this chapter, we will be concerned with the extent and logic of Lawrence's departures from a mirror image of the external events, the changing backdrop, of his life in Arabia; and with the comparative effectiveness of the two different major self-portraits, or texts of *Seven Pillars*, that he has left us. In other words, we will attempt to determine if and why Lawrence departed from strict historical truth in his account of the men and events of the Arab Revolt, and whether the 1922 or the 1926 text of *Seven Pillars* makes more powerful and moving reading. Numerous writers, among them Graves, Aldington, Weintraub, O'Donnell, Payne, and Meyers, have commented on these problems in detail, and it remains for me now only to indicate agreement or disagreement with some of their conclusions and to sum up the situation, using my own reading of the Houghton, Bodleian, and British Library manuscript material as a firm basis for judgment.

The attempt to impugn Lawrence's historical accuracy in recounting the facts of the Arab Revolt in *Seven Pillars* crystallizes in Richard Aldington's savage attack on Lawrence's whole life, including the "Lawrence legend" created by Lowell Thomas, and contains three serious charges: (1) that Lawrence told outright lies about almost every facet of the revolt and his role in it; (2) that he deliberately exaggerated Feisal's character to make him seem more epic than he actually was for various political purposes, while undercutting the Emir in more restricted writings; and (3) that he played down an assumed religious fanaticism in Feisal's army in order to make the revolt seem more a nationalistic that a religious event. If these charges could be substantiated, they would do a certain amount of damage to Lawrence's credibility an an autobiographer; the reader would feel, quite simply, that he was being lied to, and this would affect his perception of the whole work. Fortunately, we can state unequivocally that these charges have been grossly exaggerated.

Charge 1 is based on the somewhat different versions of the revolt's characters and military history that Lawrence gives in the *Secret Despatches*, the early texts of *Seven Pillars*, and the final edition. As Jeffrey Meyers notes, "Like the portrayal of the English characters, Lawrence's depiction of the Arabs in general . . . and of Feisal in particular, is much more negative in the Oxford version"[5] of *Seven Pillars*. This is to a certain extent true, but the very existence of Text III in the Bodleian, and the printing up and distribution of several copies of Text IV, the Oxford text, raises one important question: if

Lawrence was interested in completely suppressing the truth and passing off a false picture, why did he leave behind and make available during his own lifetime texts which to some degree contradict the final edition of *Seven Pillars*? The Bodleian manuscript has long been available to any scholar who wishes to see it, and was on public display in the summer of 1974, although restrictions on publishing extracts from it do exist. By the same token, the *Secret Despatches* appeared in 1939, and documents written by Lawrence remain on file both at the Bodleian and in the British government archives, where journalists Knightley and Simpson were able to read some of them in the 1960s. Even if Lawrence delayed or restricted access to these documents, he knew that they would finally be available to the prying eyes of scholars and others—and sooner rather than later, as the case has proven to be. Obviously, Lawrence was not ultimately afraid of revealing the truth as he saw it, either during his lifetime by distributing copies of the Oxford text or posthumously by leaving behind so many letters and documents. Since *Seven Pillars* does bear on the political life of an area whose fate was still being decided during the decade in which the book was published, Lawrence felt compelled to delay or restrict publication of the whole truth, which was changing every day in any case as political events took place. But the fact remains that he left behind and made available to some degree during his own lifetime his full impressions of political and military events in Arabia. This is a very foolish method of lying indeed, and we can only conclude that the highly intelligent Lawrence wanted the full truth, as he saw it, to be eventually known. Actually, as I have already demonstrated and will demonstrate, the final edition of *Seven Pillars* contains plenty of antiheroic references to English and Arab behavior, including that of Feisal, side by side with Homeric glorification.

Jeffrey Meyers' powerful argument further answers the charge of Lawrence's outright lying:

> Though Lawrence was often the only witness of the events he records, and for political and propagandistic reasons deliberately minimizes the French military role and maximizes the Arab, his account of the Revolt is essentially accurate. Apart from the official historians and the military contributors to *T. E. Lawrence By His Friends*, the direct participants in the Arab Revolt: Abdullah, Allenby, Barrow, Boyle, Bray, Bremond, Kirkbride, Meinertzhagen, Newcombe, Nouri Al-Said, Rolls, Stirling, Storrs, Vickery, Winterton and Young, as well as Djemal Pasha, Liman von Sanders and Kressenstein, have all written about their war experiences. While Barrow, Bray and

Bremond are critical of Lawrence, the accounts of both colleagues and enemies confirm his veracity.[6]

Differences of interpretation, and fuller or more restricted accounts of the facts certainly do exist, in Lawrence's own writings as well as in those of others, but the availability of Lawrence's many accounts and the reports of his colleagues, friendly and enemy, when checked against these accounts, indicate clearly that he was not "lying," and that he told an essentially accurate factual story. The reader of *Seven Pillars* can feel, and should feel, that he is being told the truth.

The following is Aldington's charge concerning the exaggeration of Feisal's character:

> The contemporary notes in the so-called *Secret Despatches* on the interviews with Feisal can hardly be reconciled with the romantic version cooked up in *Seven Pillars*. In that work, as in his post-war political propaganda, Lawrence desired to present—and with great literary skill built up—the effigy of Feisal as the warrior-prophet unerringly picked by the sagacious Lawrence and designed by Fate to lead "the Arabs" to the defeat of the Turks. . . . And Lawrence, of course, was instantly recognized by Feisal as the heaven-sent military genius to guide him. Hence the drama of their first meeting. . . .

Robert Payne also points out that Lawrence's description of his first meeting with Feisal is dramatic and glorious, while the *Arab Bulletin* report of November 18, 1916, on Lawrence's first view of Feisal only reveals disappointment with his unreasonableness. In fact, the November 18 despatch does state only that Lawrence slept well "after dining and arguing with Feisal (who was most unreasonable) for hours and hours."[7] What then of the dramatic description of Feisal as a Saladin quoted in my last chapter, and the conversation which reads almost too well to be true?: "[Feisal:] 'And how do you like our place here in Wadi Safra?' [Lawrence:] 'Well; but it is far from Damascus' " (*S*, 91). If we consult an *Arab Bulletin* despatch of November 26, 1916, we find Feisal described there by Lawrence as "tall, graceful, vigorous, almost regal in appearance . . . very like the monument of Richard I, at Fontevraud. He is hot tempered, proud, and impatient, sometimes unreasonable, and runs off easily at tangents."[8] Here we have clear evidence that Lawrence, very soon after meeting Feisal (and the chronological order of the despatches does not necessarily reflect the order of Lawrence's view of Feisal), saw him in the same heroic light that he felt while viewing Richard I's statue on one of his bicycle trips to France in 1907 (*L*, 50–51), and which fully merits the description and conversation given in *Seven Pillars* (*S*, 91). At the very same moment, he sees the bad side of Feisal's character and reports it in the verbatim language that he uses in *Seven Pillars:* "He showed himself hot-tempered and sensitive, even unreasonable, and he ran off soon on tangents" (*S*, 97). At the very worst, Lawrence is simply exercising the autobiographer's right to rearrange his material, not lying. More importantly, Lawrence's critics do not give him credit for Keats' "negative capability," the ability to hold two contradictory ideas in his mind at the same moment, and to credit each of them equally, although this is one of the keys to his character. As we have already seen, Lawrence is sincerely divided down the middle on the heroic and antiheroic aspects of his adventures.

It is true that Lawrence grew more disenchanted with Feisal as the revolt progressed, and as he himself grew more unhappy with his role in it, but here again we find an overt stripping of the veil of romance in the final edition of *Seven Pillars* itself, in which Feisal appears in the chapter analyzing heroism as a "picture-man . . . hidden in his tent, veiled to remain our leader: while in reality he was nationality's best servant, its tool, not its owner. Yet in the tented twilight nothing seemed more noble" (*S*, 547). Just as Lawrence dissects his own heroic image, so he reassesses Feisal's in the same piercing light, and despite his own romantic desire to see only the appearance, ends up reporting the reality. So the truth is reported in the final edition of *Seven Pillars* itself, which does not differ from the *Secret Despatches,* or the earlier texts, as much as some critics have made out. The *close* reader finds in the final edition an essentially accurate expression of Lawrence's feelings about Feisal, Beduin ways, and blundering Englishmen.

Is Lawrence correct in reporting no religious fanaticism in Feisal's army in *Seven Pillars?* Rightly or wrongly, he insists on this point in his letters as well: "I don't believe in any form of religious revival in the Western Islamic countries. Their present passion for nationality has driven out their former fanatical interest in creeds . . ." (*L*, 400). Lawrence did underestimate the success and power of the orthodox Wahabi movement, which was a religious revival; but this is a sincere error of judgment. On the whole and in particular about Feisal's movement, he seems to have been right. Jean Beraud-Villars questions Lawrence's veracity in this respect:

He speaks of religion with much skill at the beginning of his book, but in a general way that removes from it all actuality; in reality he never dared to tackle the problem, saying once and quite incidentally that he had not come across any fanaticism in the Hejaz, and that the profundity of national sentiments dominated religious preoccupations. He knew quite well how untrue this statement was. In Islam, the Faith is never forgotten: it colours all life and all action, and comes before anything else. [9]

In fact, Lawrence's view of Feisal's modernism vis-à-vis religion is fully substantiated by a speech of the Emir in which he declared that "We are Arabs . . . before being Moslems, and Muhammad is an Arab before being a prophet." The more one reads Lawrence, the more one is convinced that at least as far as the facts of the revolt go, Lawrence wrote as a literary autobiographer rather than the master huckster which Aldington tried to make of him. The reader of *Seven Pillars* receives an essentially sincere account of the revolt through the eyes of a man whose "negative capability" allowed him to believe and present contradictory ideas all at once.

In the manner of Doughty, Lawrence as artistic autobiographer has selected, embroidered, and heightened true events to make them dramatic. He gives clear testimony to a view of historical writing that would permit such emphasis in a letter of December, 1927, to Lionel Curtis:

One of the ominous signs of the time is that the public can no longer read history. The historian is retired into a shell to study the whole truth; which means that he learns to attach insensate importance to documents. The documents are liars. No man ever yet tried to write down the entire truth of any action in which he has been engaged. All narrative is parti pris. . . . We know too much, and use too little knowledge. (*L*, 559)

And to George Bernard Shaw he wrote in 1928 that "*The Seven Pillars* was an effort to make history an imaginative thing. It was my second try at dramatizing reality" (*L*, 603). (The "first try" was a projected work bearing the same title as *Seven Pillars* and whose subject was seven cities of the Near East. Lawrence destroyed it in 1914.) Ronald Storrs gives us a clue to precisely what Lawrence meant by "dramatizing reality" in a footnote to his memoirs, *Orientations* (1914): "Lawrence's account of the voyage, particularly of our conversations, is heightened by the use of what *The Thousand Nights and a Night* calls *Lisan al-hal*, the 'tongue, of the state or occasion;' i.e., the language deemed appropriate to the characters or circumstances." Thucydides, probably the greatest historian who ever lived, makes use of a similar expression to describe the speeches he puts into the mouths of political and military figures in his *Peloponnesian War,* and yet no one has taxed him with inaccuracy. In 1955, Storrs went even farther in vouching for Lawrence's accuracy while describing his dramatic method: "I turned to chapter VIII and found the description of Lawrence's journey with me down the Red Sea startlingly exact, except that Storrs' share of the conversation is rather puckishly tuned up. . . . I found him a touchstone and a standard of reality."[10] What departures from strict truth occur in *Seven Pillars* stem either from Lawrence's concern with the immediate political situation in the Near East or, more often, from the fact that he was an autobiographical artist rather than an "objective" historian, if such a species of being really exists.

Lawrence worked always toward heightened literary effectiveness within the framework of a basic fidelity to fact. Comparison of a passage which appeared in *The World's Work* for September, 1921, the Oxford text, and the final version reveals Lawrence's progressive growth as an artist, particularly in the writing of the many "set pieces" which appear in *Seven Pillars.* Here is the passage as it appears in *The World's Work:*

The dead lay naked under the moon, Turks are much whiter-skinned than the Arabs among whom I had been living, and these were mere boys. Close around them lapped the dark wormwood, now heavy with dew and sparkling like sea spray. Wearied in mind and body, I felt that I would rather be of this quiet company than with the shouting, restless mob farther up the valley, boasting of their speed and strength, and quarrelling over the plunder. For, however this campaign might go with its unforeseen toils and pains, death must be the last chapter in the history of every man of us.

This is the passage as it appears in the Houghton Library Oxford text, including corrections written on the page in Lawrence's handwriting:

The dead men looked wonderfully beautiful. The night was shining gently down, softening them into new ivory. Turks were white on the clothed parts of their bodies, much whiter than the Arabs among whom I was living, and these soldiers had been very young. Close round them lapped the dark wormwood, now heavy with dew, in which the ends of the moonbeams sparkled like sea-spray. They lay so pitifully on the ground, huddled anyhow in low heaps, that it seemed needful to straighten them comfortably at last. So I put them all in order, one by one, very wearied myself in mind and body, and longing to be of their quiet, not of the restless, noisy, aching mob up the valley, quarrelling over the plunder, boasting of their speed and strength to endure God knew how many toils and pains of this sort: till death, whether we succeeded or failed, wrote the last chapter in our history.

Finally, the same passage as it appears in the final edition:

The dead men looked wonderfully beautiful. The night was shining gently down, softening them into new ivory. Turks were white-skinned on their clothed parts, much whiter than the Arabs; and these soldiers had been very young. Close round them lapped the dark wormwood, now heavy with dew, in which the ends of the moonbeams sparkled like sea-spray. The corpses seemed flung so pitifully on the ground, huddled anyhow in low heaps. Surely if straightened they would be comfortably at last. So I put them all in order, one by one, very wearied myself, and longing to be one of these quiet ones, not of the restless, noisy, aching mob up the valley, quarrelling over the plunder, boasting of their speed and strength to endure God knew how many toils and pains of this sort; with death, whether we won or lost, waiting to end the history. (S, 308)

Although the literary improvement from the first passage to the second is quite marked, we might well ask whether the changes between the Oxford text passage and the final edition are at all significant. What of the differences between these texts on the whole? Which is "better?"

III *Early and Late Rembrandt*

If we extend Howarth's analogy of painting and autobiography, the Bodleian–Oxford self-portrait compares with the final version in the following way: the early portrait lacks the sureness of touch and arrangement of the later one, and contains many additional details, some enlightening, some extraneous. Because of the extra detail, both the face and the background in this early painting appear more sharply delineated and lit and the face stands out more clearly from the background. However, the sharpness of the face is only relative and it retains a certains lack of clarity. The later, final, self-portrait reveals an improvement in technique, but this new control is used to execute a deliberately more shadowy face and background which merge in a more ambiguous and symbolic chiaroscuro effect. The question is, does the perceiver prefer the sharper, blunter, more detailed but less polished and arranged early Rembrandt, or the more perfect and mysterious later one? In either case, he should realize that he will never really and fully know the poetic self-portraitist Rembrandt—or the poetic autobiographer Lawrence. Despite all the scholarly mileage that has been made out of the differences between the two textual self-portraits of Lawrence, the fact remains that S. A.'s identity is not revealed in either of them, and that the more detailed Bodleian–Oxford version does not really result in a more definitive Lawrence than the later version. In the end, the reader's textual preference becomes personal and not at all objective.

A comparison of the Bodleian–Oxford and final texts' versions of the famous Deraa incident (Chapter 80), which is inevitably selected for such a comparison, will prove just how subjective a final preference must be. Exactly what happened to Lawrence at Deraa is not yet known, but in a letter to Mrs. Charlotte Shaw he stated that he had been raped there.[11] This is not stated in the Bodleian manuscript, the printed Oxford text, or the final version. After reporting correctly that the Oxford text and to a greater degree the Bodleian manuscript contain details which "intensify the calculated cruelty and deliberate sadism" of the incident as revealed in the final version, [12] Jeffrey Meyers stresses two passages which he finds particularly significant (as does Thomas O'Donnell). About the first, Meyers writes that "the Oxford text clarifies the ambiguous statement that the Bey makes to Lawrence, the only time that he is quoted directly" and he goes on to quote the final version, with the Oxford text additions in bracketed italics:

In my despair I spoke. [*I got angry and said something to him.*] His face changed and he stood still, then controlled his voice with an effort to say significantly, "You must understand that I know [*all about you*], and it will be [*much*] easier if you do as I wish." I was dumbfounded [*by this*], and we stared silently at one another [*we waited silently for another moment, staring at one another*], while the men who felt an inner meaning beyond their experience [*while the men who had not seen an inner meaning*], shifted [*about*] uncomfortably. But it was evidently a chance shot, by which he himself did not, or would not, mean what I feared. . . . Then he sat down, and half-whispered to the corporal to take me out and teach me everything [*teach me till I prayed to be brought back*]. [The Bodleian manuscript reads *play with me till I prayed.* . . .][13]

Meyers correctly dismisses the idea that the Bey recognized T. E. Lawrence, which idea is ruled out by the "holograph summaries for chapter 80 in the Oxford text" where Lawrence states the Bey "*has no suspicion of his identity*" and does "*not suspect Lawrence is other*

than he appears." On the basis of the italicized additions, Meyers
states that "The more likely meanings of *'I know all about you'* are
that after the angry Lawrence told the Turk he was sexually de-
praved, the Turk, who had Lawrence exposed, degraded and literally
at his mercy, knew Lawrence was not what he pretended to be (an
ordinary Circassian) and recognized that Lawrence (like himself) was
a sado-masochist and perhaps a homosexual."[14] Now, Meyers makes
too great an imaginative leap on the basis of these few italicized
additions of the Oxford text. A far more likely and down-to-earth
explanation is simply that the Bey recognized that Lawrence is not as
strong as he pretends to be, and will break down and submit though
unwillingly under torture. Since Lawrence continued to cry out in
Arabic and did not betray his true identity, how could the Bey
know—as Meyers suggests—that Lawrence was not in fact "an
ordinary Circassian"?[15] In any case, both Meyers' explanation and my
own are perfectly possible to make from the final version alone,
without the Oxford additions. And, again, *no* version of *Seven Pillars*
states that Lawrence was raped, so these few details are less than
highly meaningful, and the Oxford text adds nothing essential to our
knowledge.

The second passage Meyers quotes from the Oxford text is more
explicit than the final version, but not quite as much as he makes out:

I was feeling very ill, as though some part of me had gone dead that night in
Deraa, leaving me maimed, imperfect, only half myself [The Bodleian
manuscript adds *for ever after*]. It could not have been the defilement, for no
one ever held the body in less honour that I did myself. Probably it had been
the breaking of the spirit by that frenzied nerve-shattering pain which had
degraded me to the beast level when it made me grovel to it [The Bodleian
manuscript adds *like a dog before its master*], and which had journeyed with
me since, a fascination and terror and morbid desire, lascivious and vicious,
perhaps, but like the striving of a moth towards the flame.[16]

The fact is that the final edition gives us a very clear indication of
Lawrence's masochistic tendencies: "I remembered smiling idly at
him, for a delicious warmth, probably sexual, was swelling through
me . . ." (S, 445). And the final edition contains three interesting
sentences related to this masochism which do not appear in the
earlier texts: (1) "Pain of the slightest had been my obsession and
secret terror, from a boy" (S, 446); (2) "Not that my maimed will now
cared a hoot about the Arab Revolt (or about anything but mending
itself): yet, since the war had been a hobby of mine, for custom's sake I

would force myself to push it through" (S, 447); and (3), "Their consideration (rendered at once, as if we had deserved men's homage) momently stayed me to carry the burden, whose certainty the passing days confirmed: how in Deraa that night the citadel of my integrity had been irrevocably lost" (S, 447).

The difference between the Oxford and final versions can be summed up by a comparison of the last sentence in the Oxford paragraph, about striving toward pain like a moth, and the third sentence above, about "the citadel of my integrity." The Oxford sentence is more blunt and sensational; but the sentence from the final edition, which is the last sentence in the chapter of that edition, is more beautiful rhythmically, more universal, more ambiguous, and more symbolic. It speaks not only of a single repulsive incident, but of the loss of integrity involved in the whole game of war, politics, sham acting, and cultural clash—which required Lawrence to suffer too great physical and mental torture in order to find the hidden road to be used later for an attack on Deraa and to carry through to victory a revolt which achieved less in almost every way than Lawrence had hoped.

The final version makes up in sureness of touch and greater universality what it may lack in bluntness. A simple narrative passage, the only one surviving from the destroyed Text II, reveals in its metamorphoses Lawrence's technical advance in writing:

The repeated naval bombardments had degraded the place to its original rubbish, & the contemptible remains of the dirty houses stood about in a litter lacking all the dignity of an ancient ruin: not theirs the great defiant gesture of human[ity] building facing that inevitable time whose advance years have already hacked off all the doors. (Single surviving sheet of Text II, inserted after Epilogue of Text III.)

The repeated naval bombardments had degraded the place to its original rubbish, and the poor remains of the houses stood about in a litter with none of the dignity of ancient buildings, of which durable bones face with a great defiant gesture that inevitable Time whose advancing years have already devoured their accidents. Akaba was dirty and contemptible, and the wind howled miserably across it. (Text III, Bodleian manuscript, folio 209.)

Repeated bombardments by French and English warships had degraded the place to its original rubbish, and the poor remains of the houses stood about in a litter, with none of the dignity of ancient buildings, of which the durable bones face with a great defiant gesture that inevitable Time whose advancing years have already devoured their accidents. (Text IV, Oxford text, p. 115.)

This becomes the considerably smoother statement of the final edition:

> Repeated bombardments by French and English warships had degraded the place to its original rubbish. The poor houses stood about in a litter, dirty and contemptible, lacking entirely that dignity which the durability of their time-challenging bones had conferred on ancient remains. (*S*, 314)

On the whole, Lawrence's prediction of 1923 that the final text would be "better" (*L*, 438) has been borne out. After the publication of the final version, Lawrence was never in any doubt that it surpassed artistically the Oxford text, as he wrote to Mrs. Thomas Hardy in 1927: "I'm grateful for your kindly judgement of *The Seven Pillars*. It is inevitable that people should call it less good than the 'Oxford' text, in which I first lent it you: but their judgement leaves me cold. Only I have read the two so closely as really to see the differences: and my taste in every case approved the changes" (*L*, 515). With some help from George Bernard Shaw's reading of the Oxford text, Lawrence cut verbosity and useless description. He juggled paragraphs and chapter beginnings. Many tales of the different tribes and individuals among the tribes have been dropped, along with a long personal description of Vickery and a homosexual incident between a British soldier and a Beduin (which Lawrence regarded as "beastly" but excused). The final version is thus much tighter, as Lawrence himself pointed out: "It is swifter and more pungent than the Oxford text; and it would have been improved yet more if I had had the leisure to carry the process of revision further" (*S*, 23). Robert Graves' mixed feelings probably come the closest to an accurate description of the difficulty of making a final decision between the early and later texts:

> On the whole I prefer the earliest surviving version, the so-called Oxford text, to the final printed book which was the version I first read consecutively. This is a physical rather than a critical reaction. The earlier version is 330,000 words long instead of 280,000 and the greater looseness of the writing makes it easier to read. From a critical point of view no doubt the revised version is better. It is impossible that a man like Lawrence would spend four years on polishing the text without improving it, but the nervous rigor that the revised book gave me has seemingly dulled my critical judgement.[17]

In addition to rounding off the bluntness of some observations on himself and other characters in the revolt in order to make the entire experience more symbolic and mysterious in the manner of Kinglake,

Hudson, and Doughty, all of whom mask their personalities in one way or another, Lawrence in the final edition cut down on self-conscious references to the making of a book. The passage in the final edition which begins by noting Lawrence's craving "for the power of self-expression in some imaginative form" (S, 549) is amplified in the Oxford text:

> At last accident, with perverted humour, had cast me as a man of action—and in the very height of doing I would momentarily forget my wished nature: yet always after such a crisis consciousness returned asking, how had that been done?
>
> Then I would look back at my intention, trying to find a key-word for it, in laboured sentences like these, which hid the reality, unless, perhaps, here and there, it peeped out between the lines. Chance had given me a place in the Arab Revolt, a theme epic to a direct eye and hand—and had given me a taste for the subjective, for the words to mirror our motives or feelings of the time. Whence came the indirection of my diary, and of this book built over it. (S, Oxford text, p. 231)

To the first paragraph on page 563 of the final edition, which deals with notebooks Lawrence wrote while on the march, the Oxford text adds: "The narrative hid in faint sentences, scattered through pages of opinion. Of course, my diary had to be something not harmful to others if it fell into enemy hands, but, even making this allowance, it showed clearly that my interest lay in myself, not in my activities, and four-fifths of it were useless for this re-writing" (S, Oxford text, p. 239).

After Lawrence's declaration, in the final edition that "I could not approve creation" (S, 565), apparently referring to military as well as artistic creation, the Oxford text contradicts this with the additional "Nor did I ever work my fullest, except perhaps upon some pages of this book."

In these excised passages, we see the poetic autobiographer's distress in realizing that he is more concerned with his own personality than with the external events through which he passed. He declares his intention of trying to bring his inner and outer history into more equal focus by rejecting much personal revelation in favor of outside events. And we see the degree to which he regarded himself as a creative artist, who labors to bring order and balance into his autobiography. Lawrence did not quite succeed in making his inner reactions understandable in relation to the outer public events of the revolt, as he knew himself: "I was then trying to write: to be perhaps an artist (for *Seven Pillars* had pretensions toward design, and was written with great pains as prose) or to be at least cerebral. My head was aiming to create intangible things. That's not well put: all creation is tangible. What I was trying to do, I suppose, was to carry a superstructure of ideas upon or above anything I made. Well, I failed in that" (*L*, 853). Especially after the taking of Akaba, Lawrence's personal reactions do not always follow logically from the events of the revolt. The personal element clashes with the pure epic. As a poetic autobiographer, Lawrence did not understand himself, and could only present himself on the move, in process as it were. He leaves it to the reader to create his own Lawrence, to understand for himself exactly why Lawrence felt as he did when he did. By placing the narrator-protagonist Lawrence in the context of other twentieth-century characters of the literature of British imperialism, we can illuminate and re-create his experience. We can understand the spiritual meaning of all of Lawrence's unfocussed self-portraits only by placing them on a wall with other portraits and self-portraits of his own and earlier periods.

CHAPTER 5

Seven Pillars of Wisdom: *The Two Veils*

I *The Problem*

A S narrator-protagonist in his own work, Lawrence travels the long road from Yenbo on the remote Arabian coast to the throne of Damascus, growing progressively more depressed and nerve-wracked as the military action in *Seven Pillars* swells and culminates in a successful climax. Impelled by a mysterious personal urge (his love of S. A., his rebelliousness, and his absolutism) to overcome this citadel of Turkish power, suffering mental and physical privation on the way, Lawrence finds his nerve and motive for action gone long before he takes Damascus and carries on only out of "historical ambition, insubstantial as a motive by itself" (S, 661), tasting personal defeat in military victory. The division between two political and cultural consciousnesses tears at his mind until he loses belief in English methods and honor and finally in his own capacity to control body and mind. He struggles to retain his Western, British ego in the vast ocean of the Moslem desert, loses that battle, and awakens at the end of the adventure to find himself a stranger to English and Arab alike. Where Charles Doughty and Alexander Kinglake as Victorians were able to maintain their Christian and colonial distance from the Arabs—a distance Lawrence admires from afar—and thus preserve their integrity and stability, Lawrence was considerably less successful.

To other British writers of the early twentieth century, Lawrence's was not a new story. As the product of a modern outsider in an alien and primitive environment that ultimately destroys him as a complete Englishman as well, *Seven Pillars* carries a message strikingly similar to Conrad's *Heart of Darkness*, Forster's *A Passage to India*, Orwell's *Burmese Days*, Cary's *Mister Johnson*, and other British colonial literature of our century. The process undergone by the Westerner confronting an alien environment and described in these works is roughly the following: unless the Westerner maintains his role as Sahib, or colonial ruler, he becomes involved in the other culture to the point of losing his Western identity. He returns home unable to "focus anything," in the words of Mrs. Mallowe in Kipling's "The Education of Otis Yeere," his ego destroyed. At home, he reacts violently to the truths he has learned about himself through exposure to the other culture, and becomes convinced that he has "prostituted" himself to a "brute race" (in the words of both Lawrence and Marlow in *Lord Jim*).[1] In his turn, he has imposed upon the non-Westerner his own mores, debilitating the non-Western culture in the process. The final message of all these works is that conflicts of alien cultures and political needs cannot be bridged at will, and that those who make the attempt are eliminated or maimed. In the condensed formula closing *A Passage to India*, the horses, the earth, and the rocks said " 'No, not yet,' and the sky said, 'no, not there.' "[2]

No one states the precise nature of the shock of cultures and its effect on highly sensitive twentieth-century Westerners who experience it better than Lawrence himself in the highly-tensed "Strangeness and Pain" chapter of *Seven Pillars:*

> In my case, the effort for these years to live in the dress of Arabs, and to imitate their mental foundation, quitted my of my English self, and let me look at the West and its conventions with new eyes: they destroyed it all for me. At the same time I could not sincerely take on the Arab skin: it was an affectation only. . . . Such detachment came at times to a man exhausted by prolonged physical effort and isolation. His body plodded on mechanically, while his reasonable mind left him, and from without looked down critically on him, wondering what that futile lumber did and why. Sometimes these selves would converse in the void; and then madness was very near, as I believe it would be near the man who could see things through the veils at once of two customs, two educations, two environments. (*S*, 31–32)

Because Lawrence's Arab and British veils alternate constantly, allowing him to see now through one, now through the other, he escapes madness but becomes isolated from other men and from a sense of who he is. The double pull of two cultures, combined with his fear of and contempt for the body, with its feelings of pain and touch, serves to remove Lawrence's inner self from the normal spheres of human contact. He can be sure only of his control of that inner self and his absolute subordination of his body to his will, until he finds (at Deraa) that he lacks even this certainty.

Lacking from the start a stable belief in the cultural and moral superiority of the British Raj because of his own psychological attraction to the Arabs and his knowledge of British dishonesty toward them; lacking any religious faith (as he confessed to Liddell Hart); wearing always "doubt, our modern crown of thorns" (S, 38), he could believe only in his own will and ability to straddle the fence of an increasingly dual loyalty and still remain whole mentally. Seeking to attain the simple Arab ability to believe in the revolt, he fails here too. He could satisfy his absolutist strivings among neither British nor Arabs. When this search failed him, depriving him of his identity as well, he resigned control of his life to the British army and the Royal Air Force, as recorded in *The Mint*.

Alec Dixon, a friend in the R. A. F., confirms this reading of Lawrence as a casualty of the shock of cultures; he recalls that Lawrence "talked to me of Arabia and particularly of its effect on him. Frequently he impressed on me the folly of prostituting oneself to an alien cause. (His conversation on this theme followed very closely along the lines of his preface to Doughty's *Arabia Deserta*). He had, he said, learned so well to play the Arab that he found it extremely difficult, if not painful, to return to an outlook and frame of mind that was unaffectedly Anglo-Saxon. . . . During those two years at Bovington he seemed strained and, in some moods, ten or fifteen years older than he really was: Arabia seemed to cling to him like Sinbad's old man of the sea." (*T. E. by Friends*, p. 289).

Of course, this was not the only conflict from which Lawrence suffered in Arabia. But when he sums up all the conflicting motives and torments of the will, as he does in the following document which he wrote in 1919, he always lays greatest stress on the difficulty of seeing through the two cultural veils:

I'm going to tell you exactly what my motives in the Arab affair were, in order of strength:
(i) Personal. I liked a particular Arab very much, and I thought that freedom for the race would be an acceptable present.
(ii) Patriotic. I wanted to help win the war, and Arab help reduced Allenby's losses by thousands.
(iii) Intellectual Curiosity. I wanted to feel what it was like to be the mainspring of a national movement, and to have some millions of people expressing themselves through me: and being a half-poet, I don't value material things much. Sensation and mind seem to me much greater, and the

ideal, such a thing as the impulse that took us into Damascus, the only thing
worth doing.
(iv) Ambition. You know how Lionel Curtis has made his conception of the
Empire—a commonwealth of free peoples—generally accepted. I wanted to
widen that idea beyond the Anglo-Saxon shape, and form a new nation of
thinking people, all acclaiming our freedom, and demanding admittance into
our Empire. There is, to my eyes, no other road for Egypt and India in the
end, and I would have made their path easier, by creating an Arab Dominion
in the Empire. . . . The process intended was to take Damascus, and run
it . . . as an independent ally of G[reat] B[ritain]. . . .
I'm not conscious of having done a crooked thing to anyone since I began to
push the Arab Movement, though I prostituted myself in Arab Service. For
an Englishman to put himself at the disposal of a red race is to sell himself to a
brute, like Swift's Houhynyms [*sic*]. However, my body and soul were my
own, and no one can reproach me for what I do to them: and to all the rest of
you I'm clean. (Knightley and Simpson, pp. 177-79).

Motives (i) and (iii)—Lawrence's Arab veil—balance motives (ii) and
(iv)—his British veil. Lawrence notes further that motive (i) had died
some weeks before he entered Damascus, "so my gift was
wasted. . . ." Motive (iii) was "romantic mainly, and one never
repeats a sensation. When I rode into Damascus the whole countryside was on fire with enthusiasm, and in the town a hundred thousand
people shouted my name. Success always kills the hope by surfeit."
Motive (iv), which he hoped would serve British and Arabs both, also
failed in realization when France was awarded the mandate over
Syria at the Versailles Peace Conference in 1919. Of all the motives,
only number (ii) was realized and was clearly insufficient to erase the
feeling of failure Lawrence experienced.

Any reader of *Seven Pillars* finds nothing remarkable in this list of
motives: they appear in exactly this order on the last page of the book.
The "Strangeness and Pain" chapter of the final edition, already
quoted, repeats his conclusion about prostitution in Arab service.
And throughout the book, his Arab and British sensibilities continually conflict with one another.

Despite Knightley and Simpson's attempt to portray Lawrence as a
cold-blooded British agent who cared only for "biffing the French out
of Syria" (as he wrote in a letter of 1915), and not about Arab
independence or his own honor, the evidence they provide inadver-
tently refutes their point. The accept the above document as
genuine. In it, we read clearly that only one of Lawrence's four stated
motives directly and unqualifiedly involves purely British interests;

he also appears to have had more on his mind than simple hatred or suspicion of the French. The Arab status after the war as he envisioned it, while not independence in the absolute sense, represents as much independence as could be practically achieved in view of great power interests in the area, which, as Lawrence knew, would not simply evaporate: he hoped that the British would give more to the Arabs than would the French, and his idea of including an Arab part of the so-called "Coloured Empire" (as opposed to those areas of the British Empire settled by Europeans) in a final commonwealth scheme is certainly very advanced for his time. His letter to D. G. Pearman shows that Lawrence knew the age of imperialism—or at least British imperialism at any rate—was gone forever, and that he was not seeking to insure its continuation in any way: "Do make clear to your lads, whoever they are, that my objects were to save England & France too, from the follies of the imperialists, who would have us, in 1920, repeat the exploits of Clive and Rhodes. The world has passed by that point. I think, though, there's a great future for the British Empire as a voluntary association" (*L*, 578). And this is only one of many such expressions of antiimperialism emanating from Lawrence. A passage from his war diary quoted by Knightley and Simpson confirms his concern over his position as a man of honor vis-à-vis the Arabs: "We are calling them to fight for us on a lie and I can't stand it." (Knightley and Simpson, p. 92). Is this the cold-blooded declaration of an imperialist agent?

Both *Crusader Castles* and his 1911 *Diary of a Journey Across the Euphrates* (1937), a companion volume which records details of a Mesopotamian hike, reveal his deep interest and pleasure in Syria and the relations between East and West. His letters of the prewar period show a romantic pleasure in Syria as well as hope for the Arabs. In 1912, he writes: "I am very glad you got to Baalbek and Tiberias and Damascus. All very good: but if you could have drunk rose sherbert with snow and eaten grapes in the bazaars of Aleppo in the heat! You know you have been a long time in Syria, but not with Arabs: those are people you have not met, and should" (*L*, 138). The war of 1913 between Turkey and the Balkan states draws his condemnation of Turkey as an imperial oppressor of the Arabs: "As for Turkey, down with the Turks! Their disappearance would mean a change for the Arabs, who were at any rate once not incapable of good government. One must debit them with algebra though" (*L*, 152).

In these letters and the diary, we have a Lawrence not far removed from the young and easy Kinglake. But the depth of Lawrence's experience is to transcend Kinglake's on many levels: for one thing, between Kinglake and Lawrence stands World War I, which like the khaki-clad policeman at the end of *The Sun Also Rises*, puts a total halt to romantic hopes and dreams. As one willingly *and* unwillingly involved in the deceptions attendant on the policy of the great powers, Lawrence like a Kipling Kim who has grown up to realize what he has been doing, attempts at least tactical rationalizations of his role when it comes to writing *Seven Pillars*, his prewar romanticism submerged in the dust of the Versailles Conference. On the whole, however, we can agree with Hannah Arendt's estimation of Lawrence: "Never again was the experiment of secret politics made more purely by a more decent man."

The political situation of divided aims and loyalties becomes, however, only a symptom, a tangible focus of the strain of having to see through "the veils at once of two customs, two educations, two environments," to which Lawrence attributes his occasional feeling of madness. But the political situation was spiritually difficult in itself, with Lawrence having constantly to choose between two loyalties:

> Not for the first or last time service to two masters irked me. I was one of Allenby's officers, and in his confidence: in return, he expected me to do the best I could for him. I was Feisal's adviser, and Feisal relied on the honesty and competence of my advice so far as often to take it without argument. Yet I could not explain to Allenby the whole Arab situation, nor disclose the whole British plan to Feisal. (*S*, 386)

Why, one asks, must this be so, since both Allenby and Feisal, at least in Lawrence's presentation, were honorable men? Lawrence gives legitimate political reasons at this juncture. If Feisal were to take Damascus and lose it, as Lawrence fears he would, his tribes would lose confidence and the revolt come to a halt. To have told this to Allenby, for whom even a brief occupation of Damascus by the Arabs would have been a tangible help, would have seemed foot-dragging or open partiality to the Arabs. In this case, Lawrence "decided to postpone the hazard for the Arabs' sake" (*S*, 386).

This situation occurred not once, but many times, with Lawrence sometimes keeping Allenby in the dark, and sometimes Feisal. But more corrosive than any tactical political or military skepticism is Lawrence's clear suspicion—justified by the adoption of the Sykes-Picot treaty of 1916 and Lawrence's indirect knowledge of it—that the Arabs are sacrificing for nothing, since France will receive the mandate over Syria:

The Arab Revolt had begun on false pretences. To gain the Sherif's help our Cabinet had offered, through Sir Henry McMahon, to support the establishment of native governments in parts of Syria and Mesopotamia, 'saving the interests of our ally, France.' The last modest clause concealed a treaty (kept secret, till too late, from McMahon, and therefore from the Sherif) by which France, England, and Russia agreed to annex some of these promised areas, and to establish their respective spheres of influence over all the rest. (S, 275)

Historians argue the facts of the Sykes-Picot treaty and Lawrence's claims about it even today, with inconclusive results. Since we are explicating Lawrence the narrator-protagonist as he appears between the covers of *Seven Pillars*, that is, as a literary character, we are not interested in, or concerned with settling, these disputes. However, it should be pointed out that his arguments make perfect sense within the context of *Seven Pillars* itself, and are not contradictory about the Sykes-Picot treaty. Although Lawrence "had early betrayed the treaty's existence to Feisal" (S, 555), he could not tell him the full depth of his feeling that in the end, despite his best efforts, the French and not the Arabs (as "an independent ally of Great Britain") would rule Damascus: that would have ended the Arab Revolt at once, and with it Lawrence's entire bag of goals, Arab and British. Rather, he continued to hope that Feisal's "escape was to help the British so much that after peace they would not be able, for shame, to shoot him down in its fulfilment. . ." (S, 555). Needless to say, the necessity for half-truths was excruciating to an overconscientious man like Lawrence:

Rumours of the fraud reached Arab ears, from Turkey. In the East persons were more trusted than institutions. So the Arabs. having tested my friendliness and sincerity under fire, asked me, as a free agent, to endorse the promises of the British government. I had had no previous or inner knowledge of the McMahon pledges and the Sykes-Picot treaty, which were both framed by war-time branches of the Foreign Office. But, not being a perfect fool, I could see that if we won the war the promises to the Arabs were dead paper. Had I been an honourable adviser I would have sent my men home, and not let them risk their lives for such stuff. Yet the Arab inspiration was our main tool in winning the Eastern war. So I assured them that England kept her word in letter and spirit. In this confort they performed their fine things: but, of course, instead of being proud of what we did together, I was continually and bitterly ashamed. . . .

Clearly I had no shadow of leave to engage the Arabs, unknowing, in a gamble of life and death. Inevitably and justly we should reap bitterness, a sorry fruit of heroic endeavour. (S, 275–76)

Lawrence's two veils come to the fore here: on one hand, he is not a "free agent," but a British agent, and he cares most about motive (ii), winning the war against Britain's enemies. This is the same Lawrence who concedes that "for victory everything material and moral might be pawned" (*S*, 337), referring to a purely British victory. At the same moment, he sees the Arab Revolt as "heroic endeavour," and is ashamed about his false position. What we have here is the symptom, the leading edge, of a dilemma on which Lawrence sat for two years—and not the simple hypocrisy that some see in it. The problem goes much deeper: as Albert Memmi says of the position of the colonized in his fine *The Colonizer and the Colonized* (New York, 1967), "a man straddling two cultures is rarely well seated. . . ." (p. 124). One part of Lawrence, particularly the romantic part of motive (iii), sees the Arab struggle as truly heroic; another part, the British agent, is able to view that heroism as nothing more than a tool for winning the war for the British. Lawrence penetrates Arab culture to the extent that he can criticize the British with Arab eyes; but he never loses his sense of patriotism either, and can criticize the Arabs as an Englishman: thus "negative capability."

II *The Problem's Literary Results*

The very openness of Lawrence's internal conflict, the crude juxtaposition of British-Arab contradictions, demonstrates not hypocrisy, but Lawrence's very real dilemma. If he had wanted to hide the truth completely, he could have done a much better job of smoothing out the clash that runs all through the book: he surely was intelligent enough to accomplish that, to choose simply the British *or* the Arab side for glorification, and to completely suppress any contradictory evidence. But what he gives us in *Seven Pillars* is the actual internal battle he fought during the revolt, a process of mind. Life is seldom as smooth as fiction, and the autobiographical *Seven Pillars* is looser, less tightly shaped, than a novel. In life, it is possible for a man to be a patriotic British agent and also to sympathize with an alien nationality to a very deep extent without fully understanding all the dynamics of this conflict. In Lawrence's wild fluctuations from veil to veil, we have a drama at least as interesting as the more consistent products of fiction, and well presented enough to be called artistic. As Lawrence writes to Ede about this problem of all autobiographers, "the interests of truth and form differ."[3]

The political contradictions Lawrence experienced during the revolt were not reconciled at the time of the writing of *Seven Pillars;* one reason he could offer no smoothly consistent view is that the results of his work still hung in the balance of the Versailles Conference of 1919, as he explained to Frederick Manning in 1920:

Your remarks hit off very closely the obstacles that attended the delivery of *The Seven Pillars.* I was a rather clumsy novice at writing, facing what I felt to be a huge subject with hanging over me the political uncertainty of the future of the Arab Movement. We had promised them so much, and at the end wanted to give them so little. So for two years there was a dog fight, up and down the dirty passages of Downing St., and then all came out right—only the book was finished. It might have been happier, had I foreseen the clean ending. I wrote it in some stress and misery of mind.

The second complicity was my own moral standing. I had been so much of a free agent, repeatedly deciding what I (and the others) should do: and I wasn't sure if my opportunity (or reality, as I called it) was really justified. Not morally justifiable. I could see it wasn't: but justified by the standard of Lombard St. and Pall Mall. By putting all the troubles and dilemmas on paper, I hoped to work out my path again, and satisfy myself how wrong, or how right I had been. (*L,* 691–92)

The fact that Lawrence was not able to satisfy himself on this point in *Seven Pillars* (despite the footnote in the final edition in which he declares with hindsight that England was "quit of the war-time Eastern adventure, with clean hands" [*S,* 276]) grows from a drama deeper than the simply political which he has recorded. In the synopsis of the "Strangeness and Pain" chapter, he writes "The strained mentality of rebellion which infects me and still, a year afterwards, prevents my judgement" (*S,* 7). The deeper drama of cultural clash runs through his chronical account of the military events of the revolt, a clear thread.

Despite Lawrence's comment that the following quotation applies only to *The Mint,* the wide fluctuations of feeling in *Seven Pillars* indicate that it applies equally to that book: "I tie myself into knots trying to re-act everything, as I try to write it out. It's like writing in front of a looking-glass, and never looking at the paper, but always at an imaginary scene" (*L,* 624). He wrote under the immediate impact of the story as he re-created it from memory on paper: "I feel the transition from the winter war to the expedition against Damascus to be rather abrupt: but that's because of the strain we went through in the intermediate period which seemed interminable to me, and some of whose longueurs I successfully passed into print" (*L,* 383). We recall that he attributed an "indirection" to the Oxford text because it was based on the "indirection" of a chronicle diary. In the chronicle of *Seven Pillars,* we see Lawrence's feelings change from one moment to the next. Nowhere is this indirection more obvious than in his dealings with the Arabs, which change from moment to moment according to his mood. Lawrence gives us on paper the very process of his absorption into the Arab culture and way of thinking. Although this process moves in the direction of progressive Arabization until the revelation of Deraa (which we shall discuss) and the alienation of the last book, it proceeds by "two steps forward and one back," depending again on the events of the moment, but the connection is not always clear.

When such a process is described in fiction, authors usually resort to third person narration. Thus, in Nathanael West's *Day of the Locust,* Tod's pilgrimage from the Eastern establishment (symbolized by the Yale School of Art) to his spiritual rape by the city of Los Angeles and his becoming one of the crowd of "Angelinos" is told by a third-person narrator. In *The Rock Pool,* Cyril Connolly uses a third-person narrator to describe Naylor's journey from Oxford snobbishness to the washed-out viciousness of the emigre in a seedy French subculture. In a novel like *Great Expectations,* only a distancing in time permits the first-person narrator, Pip, to describe with objectivity his journey from innocence to experience. When Henry Adams (in his *Education*) or Norman Mailer (in the first section of *Armies of the Night*) seek to reveal their personalities in the context of large historical events, they choose to write "autobiography as oratory," using third-person narration to distance themselves from themselves as characters and calling themselves by their own names rather than "I". In a letter to Shaw, Lawrence himself asks: "Isn't it treated wrongly? I mean, shouldn't it be objective, without the first-person singular?" (*L,* 390).

Lawrence, on the other hand, was temperamentally unsuited to the "autobiography as oratory" and could never achieve such an objective, distanced view of himself. In *Seven Pillars,* he attempts to describe his own process of absorption in the other culture himself, in the first person, without the necessary distancing in time. It is as if he tries to lift himself by his own bootstraps, or as if Kurtz himself were to try to describe his own descent into savagery without the benefit of an objective, intermediary narrator like Marlow. To a large extent, it is impossible for any man without great distancing in time to understand the gradations by which he slips into such a process. As a difficult, poetic personality, Lawrence cannot in any case grasp his own self in its entirety—and perhaps no man can, even a man less deep and involuted than Lawrence. His chapter "Myself" is an attempt at self-analysis deliberately written in "cypher" as he wrote to Edward Garnett, and so not wholly understandable. But even if not aiming at romantic and symbolic ambiguity, Lawrence could not have analyzed himself satisfactorily.

Lawrence thus gives us the record of his day-to-day process of Arabization and involvement in the revolt, but cannot fully understand it or explain how it happened in his role as narrator. As he wrote to Vyvyan Richards, ". . . it was and is hard to write about oneself in action." (*Portrait of T. E. Lawrence*, p. 186) This Homer presents us with the raw material of what happened to Achilles in this case, but cannot interpret it for us. Lawrence could not explain to us what happened to him, or make his book "objective" by referring to analogous processes and situations, as R. P. Blackmur points out:

One barrier to satisfaction—perhaps the only barrier—was in the limiting factor of subjectivity. Lawrence wrote always about himself, the individual who, ultimately, could not cope—with nothing, no plan or frame or conception, to fit himself into to make his tale objective in immediate import. His plain ambition is, as it were, untested; he could not steer for it, whether instinctively or deliberately; which is the difference in value between his books, and his life, and the books of the "Titans" he desired so to emulate. (*Lion and Honeycomb*, p. 123)

Blackmur is right about the problem, but wrong in his literary estimate of Lawrence because he does not understand the genre of poetic autobiography in which Lawrence is writing. Poetic autobiography *should* be completely subjective, and the reader is the one who must impose the shape and meaning on the writer's personality. As Lawrence wrote to H. S. Ede, "the latter third of *Seven Pillars* is a narrative of my personal activity," (Letters to Ede, p. 11), and even before that he is truly the one and only star of the show, as he wrote Richards: "*The making of great tragedy in its being not really my triumph.* I tried to bring this out, just this side egotism, as a second note running through the book after Chapter V, and increasing slowly towards the close, but it would be a fault in scale to present the Arab Revolt mainly as a personal tragedy to me." (Richards, p. 186) Yet this is exactly what he has done, and rightly too, for *Seven Pillars* is an "introspection epic," a poetic autobiography growing out of the "autobiography of travel" tradition, and utilizes all the mysterious and symbolic tools possible for romantically veiling the personality of the one and only major character. As he writes to Lionel Curtis in 1923, "Isn't it just faintly possible that part of the virtue apparent in the book lies in its secrecy, its novelty, and its contestability?" (*L*, 417). Lawrence leaves it to us to construct, to create the exact outlines of his self-portrait, and the best way to begin is by taking a look at the self-portrait of the kind of man he was not, and knew he was not: Charles Doughty.

III *Lawrence and Doughty Revisited*

In his introduction to *Arabia Deserta,* Lawrence writes at his own modern expense and in favor of the Victorian Doughty:

We export two chief kinds of Englishmen, who in foreign parts divide themselves into two opposed classes. Some feel deeply the influence of the native people, and try to adjust themselves to its atmosphere and spirit. . . . They imitate the native as far as possible, and so avoid friction in their daily life. However, they cannot avoid the consequences of imitation, a hollow, worthless thing. . . . The other class of Englishman is the larger class. In the same circumstances of exile they reinforce their character by memories of the life they have left. In reaction against their foreign surroundings they take refuge in the England that was theirs. They assert their aloofness, their immunity, the more vividly for their loneliness and weakness. They impress the peoples among whom they live by reaction, by giving them an example of the complete Englishman, the foreigner intact.
    Doughty is a great member of the second, the cleaner class. (Introduction to *Arabia Deserta,* p. 20)

Lawrence, a man of the first, in his opinion the dirtier class, ultimately neither an Arab nor a complete Englishman, here looks with envy on the kind of traveler he could never be. But in letters he wrote to Mrs. Shaw in 1927, Lawrence reveals what he really thinks of the "second, the cleaner class" of Englishmen abroad:

Doughty really believed in his superiority to the Arabs. It was this pride that made him meek in oppression. He really believed that he held a knowledge of the truth, and that they were ignorant. He really believed that the English were better than the Arabs: that this thing was better than that thing: in fact, he really did believe in something. That's what I call an absolute. Doughty, somewhere, if only in the supremacy of Spenser, had a fixed point in his universe, and from one fixed point a moralist will, like a paleontologist, build up the whole scheme of creation. Consequently, Doughty's whole book is rooted; definitive; assured. . . . Doughty sees through his eyes, and not through the eyes of his companions. He was devoid of sympathy. . . . Such fanatic love and hatred ought not to be.[4]

In a letter written to Mrs. Shaw one month later, Lawrence again compares his relativistic viewpoint with Doughty's fixed point:

Search my book through, and you will hardly find an assertion which is not immediately qualified; and certainly not an assertion which is not eventually qualified. It's due to an absence of the fixed point from which Doughty radiated. My views are like my photographs of Jidda: the edges, even of the sharpest, are just modulated off, so that you can't put a pin point on them. Drawn, not in line, but in tone. Atmospheric. It's the difference between impressionism and the classical.[5]

In the same letter, Lawrence sums up his criticism of Doughty, the Victorian judge of the Arabs: "Who are we to judge? I don't believe even God can." In 1923, he writes about Doughty that "A bigger man would not read the *Morning Post*" (L, 438). David Garnett clarifies this comment with a footnote: "The simplicity of Doughty's patriotism, which was without reservations, was not possible to Lawrence after the Peace Conference." To this we might add that Lawrence shows no signs of this simple patriotism before the Conference, either. Because Lawrence lacks the fixed point of Victorian pride, *Seven Pillars* becomes contradictory, "atmospheric," and contains a more subtle drama than that contained in the works of Doughty and Kinglake: he traces the absorption of himself into Arab culture and his subsequent realization that he has become neither English nor Arab, that he sees the West with new eyes "which destroyed it all for me." This is not to say, however, that Lawrence becomes fully like Conrad's Kurtz and ever abandons entirely his Western identity. E. M. Forster, who knew him very well, makes this point clearly in *Abinger Harvest:*

He was, of course, devoted to the Arab cause. Yet when it triumphed he felt he had let down both his own countrymen and the foreigner by aping foreign ways, and became more English than ever. To regard him as 'gone native' is wrong. He belonged body and soul to our islands. And he should have been happier in olden days, when a man could feel surer that he was fighting for his own hearth, and this terrible modern mix-up had not begun. (p. 170)

To trace how far "this terrible modern mix-up" of cultures—also exemplified, in the case of Englishmen and Italians, in the Forster

novels *Where Angels Fear to Tread* and *A Room with a View*—and the
lack of a fixed point of cultural pride took its toll on Lawrence, we
have only to compare his view of the Arabs withDoughty's, note his
attraction to them, and then to examine the drama resulting from this
attraction.

In the chapter on Semitic religiosity, the Arabs appear to think and
see like Doughty, according to Lawrence's view of him, although
Lawrence does not make the direct connection:

> Semites had no half-tones in their register of vision. They were a people of
> primary colours, or rather of black and white, who saw the world always in
> contour. They were a dogmatic people, despising doubt, our modern crown
> of thorns. They did not understand our metaphysical difficulties, our intros-
> pective questionings. They knew only truth and untruth, belief and unbelief,
> without our hesitating retinue of finer shades. (S, 38)

Like Doughty, the Arabs see in sharp photographs, while Lawrence,
wearing the "modern crown of thorns," sees the fine gradations of
color of the impressionistic late Victorians. This passage comes
almost wholly into *Seven Pillars* from Lawrence's introduction to
Doughty's book, revealing that the connection between Doughty and
the nomads may not have been far from his mind. The Arabs are the
"least morbid of peoples, they had accepted the gift of life unques-
tioningly, as axiomatic" (S, 38). In Lawrence's preface, Doughty is
"never morbid, never introspective." Now we understand Lawrence's total inability to read or like Dickens (L, 735), who tends to
see moral issues in terms of black and white, like Doughty.

But, as much as Lawrence is unlike the Arabs, he feels a powerful
attraction to their habits of renunciation and austerity: "But at last
Dahoum drew me: 'Come and smell the very sweetest scent of all,'
and we went into the main lodging, to the gaping window sockets of
its eastern face, and there drank with open mouths of the effortless,
empty, eddyless wind of the desert, throbbing past. . . . 'This,' they
told me, 'is the best: it has no taste' " (S, 40). Lawrence's identification of himself with this passage is evident in its highly colored aesthetic style and the mention of Dahoum, whom he names openly
nowhere else in the book.

The God of the Beduin actually surpasses the cold God of Christianity because he is more familiar, in Lawrence's presentation:

> The Beduin could not look for God within him: he was too sure that he was
> within God. He could not conceive anything which was or was not God, Who

alone was great; yet there was a homeliness, an everyday-ness of this climatic Arab God, who was their eating and their fighting and their lusting, the commonest of their thoughts, their familiar resource and companion, in a way impossible to those whose God is so wistfully veiled from them by despair of their carnal unworthiness of Him and by the decorum of formal worship. (S, 40–41)

Further, the Beduin's

sterile experience robbed him of compassion and perverted his human kindness to the image of the waste in which he hid. Accordingly he hurt himself, not merely to be free, but to please himself. There followed a delight in pain, a cruelty which was more to him than goods. The desert Arab found no joy like the joy of voluntarily holding back. He found luxury in abnegation, renunciation, self-restraint. (S, 41)

Lawrence, swinging such a people "on an idea as on a cord," brought up a great wave, "till it reached its crest, and toppled over and fell at Damascus" (S, 42–43). He expresses the hope that "The wash of that wave, thrown back by the resistance of vested things [read the French] will provide the matter of the following wave, when in fullness of time the sea shall be raised once more" (S, 43). The heightened style, comprising rich metaphors and crests of waves of excitement, indicates Lawrence's pleasure in these features of his Arab "veil." Later, he expands the idea of renunciation to include servitude, another of his own predilections: "Servitude, like other conduct, was profoundly modified to Eastern minds by their obsession with the antithesis between flesh and spirit. These lads took pleasure in subordination; in degrading the body; so as to throw into greater relief their freedom in equality of mind: almost they preferred servitude as richer in experience than authority, and less binding in daily care" (S, 466). Lawrence, attracted to the Beduin—as opposed to the town Arabs—in some ways, but still unable to see in terms of black and white like them, paints a largely favorable picture; Doughty, who does see in those terms, paints a largely unfavorable picture: he collides head-on with those who think like himself but hold different views. Unlike Lawrence, he could never praise Allah at the expense of his God. In Arabia, he sees only "the bitterness and blight of a fanatical religion, in every place" (*Arabia Deserta, I*, p. 33). Christianity "were fain to cast her arms about the human world, sealing all men one brotherhood with a virginal kiss of meekness and charity," but "the Mohammedan chain-of-credulities is an elation of the soul, breathing of God's favour only to the Moslemin: and shrewdness out of her cankered bowels to all the world besides" (*Arabia Deserta*, II, pp. 406-7). Like Kinglake, Doughty may criticize Christians but he never admits Islam to a spiritual equality with Christianity. Instead of attraction to or understanding of Beduin fatalism and renunciation, it offends his Victorian ideal of progress: "the nomads lie every day of their lives upon their hungry maws, waiting for the mercy of Ullah: this is the incurious misery of human minds faint with the hunger of generations grown barren in the desert" (*Arabia Deserta*, I, p. 448). It is no wonder that Doughty's amazingly liberal contemporary, Richard Burton, a greater Arabist than either Doughty or Lawrence, decided that Doughty's book taught, if nothing else, "the need for a certain pliancy in opinion, religious and political, in a traveller."[6]

Lawrence, unlike Doughty, was a post-Christian, and he was divided over the value of technology, using new devices to destroy the railroad which was bringing progress into the Hejaz. In replying to Herbert Read's criticism of *Seven Pillars,* Lawrence writes: "I entirely repudiate his suggestion that one race is better than another. This is the purest jingoism and Morning Postliness" (*L,* 550). This remark applies equally to the difference between Lawrence and Doughty. Rather than a sweeping condemnation of Doughty, who was a victim of his time and a certain conditioned mentality, Lawrence's criticism shows his own modernistic relativity, a vision which cost him dearly.

IV   *The Colonizer Who Refused*

In a telling passage that was eliminated from the final edition, Lawrence compares himself to Vickery, another Englishman of "The second, the cleaner class," like Doughty. Lawrence says that he keeps apart from the Arabs in spirit, though not in manner, because he fears that the Arabs would see through the "legend of our greatness." Vickery, on the other hand, feels condescension toward the "natives," rather than self-deprecation before them:

Vickery tended to be a regal boon companion, and risked earning their contempt by showing an unconscious condescension. To this society of Sheiks and Sherifs with their sense of personal dignity, he came fresh from years in Government circles, where he had experienced servility and rebellious insolence, but never friendship. His examples of native authority had been clerks or officials, not men born to power, and the veil of office as subtle and impermeable as our veil of flesh, lay between him and the people. For this difficulty the East preferred stupid Englishmen as governors. The brilliant sometimes guessed, and then were dangerous, but it salved a little the hurt native self-respect to fool the others. The first meeting in native dress with an Englishman, witnessing that awful blankness in his eye, which saw, not a fellow man, but a landscape or local colour, had illuminated my dark places. Use would either impress his opinion to the ruin of my self-respect, or it would have brought resentful violence in assertion of a common humanity. It led me to a constant reading of the Houhynyms, whether I was dressed Arab or English fashion, but that grace was because I inhabited the same body under another envelope, and could always laugh. (S, Oxford text, p. 55).

Albert Memmi points out that "another sign of the colonized's depersonalization is what one might call the mark of the plural. The colonized is never characterized in an individual manner; he is entitled only to drown in an anonymous collectivity" (Memmi, p. 85). Like the author of *Black Like Me,* who has his skin dyed black in order to experience the feelings of a Negro in the South, Lawrence as Englishman had direct personal experience of what it felt like to be condescended to by other Englishmen who thought he was an Arab, as this passage shows. How well he understands the feeling of an Arab in this position, who is regarded as a "landscape or local colour," is apparent. In Vickery, Lawrence has described the people in the Club of Anglo-Indians that Fielding confronts in *A Passage to India*. Like Fielding, he sees too deeply to practice their prejudices, at this early stage; later, like Fielding, he is to find himself alienated from the other culture, and becomes more English than ever, as Forster points out. Here Lawrence can laugh at the comic situation by which one nation can regard itself as Houhynyms and everyone else as Yahoos. Later, Lawrence says that he has prostituted himself to Yahoos, in the form of the Arabs.

After noting the incongruity of the Australian Lewis, who feels superior to all brown men although "he was browner by far than my new followers," Lawrence launches into a precise description of Rahail ("a free-built, sturdy fellow, too fleshy for the life we were to lead, but for that the more tolerant of pains. His face was high-coloured; his cheeks a little full and low-pouched, almost pendent" [S, 346]), proving that he does not see the Arabs as "local color," but as individuals. All his Arab portraits reveal this same particularity, especially in physical features. The fact that Lawrence does not portray anyone—Arab or British, including himself—in the book as a fully rounded character has more to do with his artistic aims and abilities than with his spiritual outlook on the Arabs, contrary to what Thomas O'Donnell claims. He notices clearly physical differences, but never enters fully into the mind of anyone but himself, and fails there as well.

Like Fielding, Lawrence sees past the barriers between colonizer and colonized, and finds the situation humiliating when not openly humorous: "It was humiliating to find that our book-experience of all countries and ages still left us prejudiced like washerwomen, but without their verbal ability to get on terms with strangers" (S, 346). We should remember that Lawrence is of Irish ancestry and naturally feels more sympathy with the colonized than do Forster's Turtons, for example, although not more than Fielding. How little Lawrence subscribed in thought or action to the mentality of the colonialist shows plainly in a passage remarkable for its insight:

> Englishmen, accustomed to greater returns, would not, and indeed, could not, have spent the time, thought and tact lavished every day by sheikhs and emirs for such meagre ends. Arab processes were clear, Arab minds moved as logically as our own, with nothing radically incomprehensible or different, except the premiss: there was no excuse of reason, except our laziness or ignorance, whereby we could call them inscrutable or Oriental, or leave them misunderstood. (S, 220)

Lawrence's dilemma is indeed strange. He leads an anticolonial movement against the Turks, who have colonized the Arabs for centuries, and comes to sympathize more and more with the Arab antipathy to Turkish oppression; yet, as the agent of a British movement which will culminate in European domination of the Arabs, he must act out the role of colonialist. Seen in this light, Lawrence winds up in what Memmi describes as the position of the "colonizer who refuses":

> A colonizer who rejects colonialism does not find a solution for his anguish in revolt. If he does not eliminate himself as a colonizer, he resigns himself to a position of ambiguity. If he spurns that extreme measure, he contributes to the establishment and confirmation of the colonial relationship. It is under-standable that it is more convenient to accept colonization and to travel the whole length of the road from colonial to colonialist.
>
> A colonialist is, after all, only a colonizer who agrees to be a colonizer. By making his position explicit, he seeks to legitimize colonialization. This is a more logical attitude, materially more coherent than the tormented dance of the colonizer who refuses and continues to live in a colony. (Memmi, p. 45)

We cannot dismiss Lawrence's worries over this situation as the superficial and hypocritical complaints of one who has deeper psychological problems, or *Seven Pillars* reduces to a casebook of abnormal psychology when in fact it is a very brilliant and valuable document of all the many problems of the spirit attendant on World War I. The "colonizer who refuses" is in the position of seeing through two veils at once. Lawrence knows he is in this position:

> You guessed rightly that the Arab appealed to my imagination. It is the old, old civilisation, which has refined itself clear of household gods, and half the trappings which ours hastens to assume. The gospel of bareness in materials is a good one, and it involves apparently a sort of moral bareness too. They think for the moment, and endeavour to slip through life without turning corners or climbing hills. In part it is a mental and moral fatigue, a race trained out, and to avoid difficulties they have to jettison so much that we think honourable and grave: and yet without in any way sharing their point of view, I think I can understand it enough to look at myself and other foreigners from their direction, and without condemning it. I know I'm a stranger to them, and always will be; but I cannot believe them worse, any more than I could change their ways. (*L,* 244)

Lawrence was fully capable of seeing the British, including himself, with Arab eyes; his position forced him to do so. He must himself seek out Gasim, his lost servant, for

> My shirking the duty would be understood, because I was a foreigner: but that was precisely the plea I did not dare set up, while I yet presumed to help these Arabs in their own revolt. It was hard, anyway, for a stranger to influence another people's national movement, and doubly hard for a Christian and a sendentary person to sway Moslem nomads. I should make it impossible for myself if I claimed, simultaneously, the privileges of both societies. (*S,* 254)

Lawrence is like a white man who is somehow placed in the position of aiding a "black power" movement; he constantly charts his forced immersion into Arab mores and the effect this had on him, without totally understanding it.

Knightley and Simpson quote Lawrence's *Twenty Seven Articles,* a cultural primer on the Arabs that he wrote for the benefit of British servicemen in the Near East, as evidence of his manipulation of Arab customs for his own ends, in order to demonstrate that he cared only for these "sinister" ends ("biffing the French out of Syria") and not for the Arab Movement at all. Yet they ignore the implications of the clear warning he gives at the end of Article 20:

If you wear Arab things at all, go the whole way. Leave your English friends and customs on the coast, and fall back on Arab habits entirely. It is possible, starting thus level with them, for the European to beat the Arabs at their own game, for we have stronger motives for our action, and put more heart into it than they. If you can surpass them, you have taken an immense stride towards complete success, but the strain of living and thinking in a foreign and half-understood language, the savage food, strange clothes, and still stranger ways, with the complete loss of privacy and quiet, and the impossibility of ever relaxing your watchful imitation of the others for months on end, provide such an added stress to the ordinary difficulties of dealing with the Bedu, the climate, and the Turks, that this road should not be chosen without serious thought. (Knightly and Simpson, p. 70)

In the end, Lawrence is as much manipulated by Arab society as he manipulates individual Arabs: hence his final feeling of having "prostituted" himself. Neither Fielding nor Lawrence succeeds in bridging the cultures in the end.

V *Foundations of Cultural Clash: Chapters 1–7*

The very title, "Seven Pillars of Wisdom," of Lawrence's book, reveals the complex mixture of East and West that make up its contents. The Bible is both an Eastern and Western book, and the phrase that supplies Lawrence's title comes directly from Prov. 9:1, "Wisdom hath builded her house, she hath hewn out her seven pillars." There are other biblical resonances as well, for in Deut. 1:13 and Exod. 18:21 leaders of the people of Israel are said to have *seven* qualities: wisdom, understanding, experience, ability, fear of God, trustworthiness, and incorruptibility. And we must not forget the "Five Pillars of Faith" of the Moslem religion either. Further, as Lawrence points out (*L*, 514), the phrase implies "a complete edifice of knowledge" because "The figure 'seven' implies completeness in the Semitic languages." Lawrence is certainly right about this, for in Hebrew seven is "sheva," and full, "save'ah" derives from the same root. On the other hand, the degree to which Lawrence felt he failed in building this edifice according to the seven desirable qualities is indicated in the subtitle, "A triumph," which is certainly ironic if one considers the bitter personal as opposed to triumphant military events.

Similarly, the motto "the sword also means clean-ness and death" is a complex multilingual pun, for "Feisal" in Arabic means sword. The introductory poem shares the same exotic, un-English fullness of phrase and aspiration, and in it the revolt is compared to "an inviolate house" based on seven pillars of freedom, which is however shattered "unfinished" in this case by Lawrence's own will as a monument to his unfulfilled love of the dead S. A. In the epilogue to the book, which is couched in the same high romantic tone as the title, motto, and introductory poem, Lawrence discloses that the revolt was finished because of "the exhaustion of my main springs of action," rather than by his willed choice. The chapter on "Strangeness and Pain" echoes this high romantic tone which on the one hand glorifies exotic Eastern adventures and on the other is undercut by its content: the toll his adventures took on Lawrence. The feeling throughout this introductory matter is of an attraction for the East, but also an undercutting realization that the revolt did not end for Lawrence as it should have, that his Western self has brought him back down to earth even as he writes in as highly colored a style as possible.

The mixed tone of this introductory but retrospective material appears most clearly in the introductory chapter of the Oxford text, which was removed from the final edition on the advice of G. B. Shaw but then replaced in all British, but not American editions of *Seven Pillars:*

> I meant to make a new nation, to restore a lost influence, to give twenty millions of Semites the foundation on which to build an inspired dream-palace of their national thoughts. . . .
>   . . . All the subject provinces of our Empire to me were not worth one dead English boy. If I have restored to the East some self-respect, a goal, ideals: if I have made the standard rule of white over red more exigent, I have fitted those peoples in a degree for the new commonwealth in which the dominant races will forget their brute achievements, and white and red and yellow and brown and black will stand up together without side-glances in the service of the world. (*S,* Oxford text, p. 1)

When Lawrence speaks of making "a new nation" and "an inspired dream-palace" his prose becomes high-romantic, revealing the Lawrence who is the "music-maker, maker of dreams" of the O'Shaughnessy "Ode"; when he speaks of "self-respect," the "service of the world," and most of all "one dead English boy," he reveals the Kiplingesque British schoolmaster in him: we have both Arab and

British patriotism side by side here, the romantic Arab tone somewhat higher pitched and more exotic, the British flatter and more
clichéd but still powerfully felt and expressed.

In this introductory chapter, Lawrence's retrospective balance
between his cultural and political loyalties is more evenly stated than
in the rest of the opening book of *Seven Pillars,* in which he describes
Arab mores and religion and the political history of the revolt in the
most sympathetic terms. He takes the position of the colonized
people, understands their psychological defenses against the colonizer, and almost projects himself into Arab shoes: "The Arabs
would not give up their rich and flexible tongue for crude Turkish. . . . The knowledge that his religion was his own, and that only
he was perfectly qualified to understand and practice it, gave every
Arab a standard by which to judge the banal achievements of the
Turk" (*S,* 45). The Turks even appear corrupt from within: "Medical
examination of some batches of Turkish prisoners found nearly half of
them with unnaturally acquired venereal disease. . . . The Turkish
peasantry of Anatolia were dying of their military service" (*S,* 56). In
contrast, Arab youths "slake one another's few needs in their own
clean bodies" (*S,* 30). Turkish venereal disease—and not homosexuality, except when it amounts to rape—becomes an emblem of corrupt
rule. The idea is that Feisal's movement (which represents "clean-
ness" and romantic death, according to the motto) and Lawrence's
love for S. A. are essentially pure-hearted, idealistic phenomena
while Turkish colonial rule is corrupt in practice and conception.

In contrast with Arab "cleanness," the English themselves appear
corrupt in Lawrence's opening portraits of the men with whom he
worked in Cairo, especially in the Oxford text, as Meyers (and
O'Donnell) correctly point out, but the final edition's characteriza-
tions are critical enough. Ronald Storrs appears in the final edition as
one who could have achieved more brilliantly "had he been able to
deny himself the world, and to prepare his mind and body with the
sternness of an athlete for a great fight" (*S,* 57). The portraits of all the
"Intrusives" of the Arab Bureau except Hogarth, Lawrence's mentor
and the first in a series of father figures, are carefully balanced
between praise and criticism. Lawrence brings up the specters of the
great British failures at Gallipoli and Kut and (until the arrival of
Allenby) scarcely sings an epic of British arms. Sir Archibald Murray
and his chief of staff, Lynden Bell, come off as badly as the slow-
witted and blundering Turkish commanders Lawrence later derides.

He closes this introductory book with a clear statement of his spiritual—rather than coldly political or military—involvement in the Arabs' revolt against Turkey:

> . . . I justified myself by my confidence in the success of the Arab Revolt if properly advised. I had been a mover in its beginning; my hopes lay in it. The fatalistic subordination of a professional soldier (intrigue being unknown in the British army) would have made a proper officer sit down and watch his plan of campaign wrecked by men who thought nothing of it, and to whose spirit it made no appeal. *Non nobis, Domine.* (S, 63)

VI   *To Akaba: Books 1–4 (Chapters 8–54)*

In the beginning of Book 1, which details Lawrence's initiation into the adventure, "the heat of Arabia came out like a drawn sword and struck us speechless" (S, 65). This unfamiliar heat signals the beginning of the conflict between the Westerner and the new environment. Like the fever that Marlow experiences in his descent into "the heart of darkness," the heat of Arabia is "the playful paw-strokes of the wilderness, the preliminary trifling before the more serious onslaught which came in due course";[7] although Jidda was "a remarkable town," its "atmosphere was oppressive, deadly" (S, 72–73). In a symbolic touch worthy of Conrad, Lawrence uses the captured Turkish band's rendition of the German "Hymn of Hate" to introduce the theme of the jumble of cultures: "no one could recognize a European progression in it at all" (S, 75). But Lawrence, at least in the Oxford text, enjoys it nonetheless: "There was a satisfying ring in that tune played in Jidda to the leaders of the new revolt in Islam by the captured band of the Turkish governor of the holy places" (S, Oxford text, p. 17).

Lawrence wrote Edward Garnett that his best writing is to be found in the long ride up to Feisal that follows (L, 513), and in fact it contains some of the best travel writing on record. Romantic hope and diction infuse the whole account; the new scenery, language, and customs become delightful toys for Lawrence, despite the hint of unknown danger beneath the surface. He mounts Sherif Ali's "own splendid riding camel," whose every detail of embroidery he notes with admiration and pleasure. He travels the Mecca pilgrim road, "down which, for uncounted generations, the people of the north had come to visit the Holy City . . . and it seemed that the Arab revolt might be in a sense a return pilgrimage, to take back to the north, to Syria, an ideal for an ideal, a belief in liberty for their past belief in revelation" (S, 78). In the manner of Doughty, Lawrence transposes contemporary Arabic into archaic English, as in his conversation with Tafas. But always under the interest and beauty lurks a sinister note: "The particles of sand were clean and polished, and caught the blaze of sun like little diamonds in a reflection so fierce, that after awhile I could not endure it" (*S*, 83).

At this point, Lawrence still "had no sense of how to ride," and feels the strangeness of his surroundings at every step, for "The last two years I had spent in Cairo, at a desk all day or thinking hard in a little over-crowded office full of distracting noises. . . . In consequence the novelty of the change was severe, since time had not been given me to gradually accustom myself to the pestilent beating of the Arabian sun, and the long monotony of camel pacing" (*S*, 84). He "was always falling asleep in the saddle, to wake a few seconds later suddenly and sickeningly, as I clutched by instinct at the saddle post to recover my balance. . . . It was too dark, and the forms of the country were too neutral, to hold my heavy-lashed, peering eyes" (*S*, 85). He can eat only a little of the Arabs' unleavened dough cake "on this, my first attempt." Yet he is interested "to find myself in a new country," in which the colors are "joyously blended" (*S*, 86).

Lawrence comes on Feisal suddenly: "I felt at first glance that this was the man I had come to Arabia to seek—the leader who would bring the Arab revolt to full glory" (*S*, 91). There follows the exotic and embroidered description of Feisal. In the best colored tones of Anglo-Arabian writing, Lawrence has built suspense to this meeting by means of rich metaphors and detail, and thus justifies it artistically. His attraction to the adventure comes through plainly on these pages.

Lawrence now gives an account of the "bitter taste of the Turkish mode of war," as he creates sympathy for the Arabs as an oppressed people. He makes no attempt to hide Feisal's unreasonable qualities, but in sum, "if he had the strength to realize his dreams he would go very far, for he was wrapped up in his work and lived for nothing else" (*S*, 97). To the tribes, Feisal like his father is "heroic" (*S*, 98). But Feisal suspects British intentions:

"You see," he explained, "we are now of necessity tied to the British. We are delighted to be their friends, grateful for their help, expectant of our future profit. But we are not British subjects. We would be more at ease if they were not such disproportionate allies. . . ."

"I am not a Hejazi by upbringing; and yet, by God, I am jealous for it. And though I know the British do not want it, yet what can I say, when they took the Sudan, also not wanting it? They hunger for desolate lands, to build them up; and so, perhaps, one day Arabia will seem to them precious. Your good and my good, perhaps they are different, and either forced good or forced evil will make a people cry with pain. Does the ore admire the flame which transforms it?" (S, 99–100)

After this eloquent presentation of the Arab case against colonialism through the mouth of Feisal, Lawrence's British veil suddenly swings into place. He comments favorably on the weakness of the Arabs and their natural antipathy to the centralized state: "Were it otherwise, we should have had to pause before evoking in the strategic centre of the Middle East new national movements of such abounding vigour" (S, 101). Negative capability: Lawrence himself writes up an attack on British imperialism and then in the next breath speaks as a British agent. Here "we" refers to the British; later, as he becomes more involved in the revolt, "we" will signify the Arabs. The story of *Seven Pillars* is largely that of this shift in the meaning of "we," of the transformation of Lawrence to "Aurens" and back again, and finally in *The Mint* to Ross and then to Shaw. Whenever the British side of Lawrence's dual role appears, his upper lip stiffens and his prose shows it by becoming flatter, less exalted, less personal. He must switch his eyes "straight to my brain" in his British capacity, "that I might note a thing or two the more clearly by contrast with the former mistiness" (S, 102). His romantic self is impressionistic. In his British mood, he sees clearly and stands apart from "romantics": "I believed in the Arab movement, and was confident, before ever I came, that in it was the idea to tear Turkey to pieces. . . . By noting down something of these romantics in the hills about the Holy Cities I might gain the sympathy of Cairo . . ." (S, 102). Yet a fight for freedom appeals to him, even in his cooler British mood: "There was among the tribes in the fighting zone a nervous enthusiasm common, I suppose, to all national risings, but strangely disquieting to one from a land so long delivered that national freedom had become like water in our mouths, tasteless" (S, 105–106).

Lawrence leaves Feisal, having been attracted to the movement with one side of his personality, but having finally assessed it in purely British terms. But when he returns to "civilization," in the form of the ship *Suva*, captained by Boyle, a strange thing happens: he already finds himself identified as less than British by an Anglo-Arabian:

He had done much in the beginning of the revolt, and was to do much more for the future: but I failed to make a good return impression. I was travel-stained and had no baggage with me. Worst of all I wore a native head-cloth, put on as a compliment to the Arabs. Boyle disapproved.

Our persistence in the hat (due to a misunderstanding of the ways of heat-stroke) had led the East to see significance in it, and after long thought their wisest brains concluded that Christians wore the hideous thing that its broad brim might interpose between their weak eyes and the uncongenial sight of God. So it reminded Islam continually that God was miscalled and misliked by Christians. The British thought this prejudice reprehensible (quite unlike our hatred of a head-cloth) one to be corrected at any price. If the people would not have us hatted, they should not have us any way. Now as it happened I had been educated in Syria before the war to wear the entire Arab outfit when necessary without strangeness, or sense of being socially compromised. The skirts were a nuisance in running up stairs, but the head-cloth was even convenient in such a climate. (S, 109)

Lawrence's desire to wear Arab kit goes beyond mere playing to the Arab gallery, as the photographs he posed for Lowell Thomas reveal: like the liberal antiimperialist Blunt, he enjoyed the romance of Arab gear and even found it useful. Because of this liberality, he begins his adventures at some distance from the overt colonizers of "the second class" like Boyle.

In the following books, Lawrence charts his forced immersion into Arab mores and even thought processes, abetted by his own romantic desire for strangeness. Thus, he agrees "very gladly" when Feisal asks him to wear Arab robes while in camp (S, 126). In the description of the "rather splendid and barbaric" march on Owais, it is "we" who "filled the valley to its banks with our flashing stream," referring to himself and the Arabs; he appears on Sharraf's left dressed in "white and scarlet" (S, 140–141). Sir Mark Sykes realized the strong strain of Arab sympathy in Lawrence. As early as July 22, 1917, he speaks of eventual Arab independence under Entente tutelage and adds about Lawrence: "Let him consider this as he hopes for the people he is fighting for." (Knightly and Simpson, p. 83).

During the march on Wejh, Lawrence feels gloriously happy: "the freshness of the day and the life and happiness of the Army gave inspiration to the march and brought the future bubbling out of us without pain" (S, 149). In the Oxford text, he speaks at this point of the "moral greatness of the march up-country" (S, Oxford text, p. 53). He even sacrifices his beloved privacy for the revolt, because "the work suffered by the creation of such a bar between the leaders and the men" (S, 157). The characterization of Sherif Nasir has the ring of chivalric title: "He was the opener of roads, the forerunner of Feisal's movement . . . and from the beginning to end all that could be told of him was good" (S, 160). At the same time, he can speak with pleasure of "Englishmen and Arabs" dining and discussing together (S, 144).

When he discusses the Negroes in Feisal's camp, we get an interesting passage which Aldington cites as an example of what he terms Lawrence's "feeling of racial superiority": "It was as with the negroes, tom-tom playing themselves to red madness each night under the ridge. Their faces, being clearly different from our own, were tolerable; but it hurt that they should possess exact counterparts of all our bodies" (S, 171). Instead of blind racism, this passage actually indicates more clearly than practically any other in the book Lawrence's shock of immersion into a foreign culture. Compare Marlow's statement on tribesmen in Africa: "It was unearthly and the men were—no they were not inhuman . . . that was the worst of it—this suspicion of their not being inhuman." (Heart of Darkness, p. 31). In his brilliant study of the effect of empire on late nineteenth-century British literature, The Wheel of Empire, Alan Sandison says this about the Conrad passage above:

Confrontation with the primitive, unorganized native discloses a horrible and unsuspected affinity between him and the sophisticated alien which makes clear just how much of an assumption, how much of a carefully erected, entirely superficial thing, individual identity is. One's own moral organization depends on the degree of social organization experienced environmentally. And when this is exposed as brutally as it is by these primitive people the whole basis of integrity is undermined. (p. 128).

What Lawrence experiences here is not unusual to his own psyche, though, characteristically, he thinks it is: the Negroes call up "something hurtful to my pride." In fact, this experience is common to all those Englishmen who venture into unknown and more primitive environments in British imperial literature; and the result, as Sandison notes, is a threat to their identities. One recognizes oneself in the tribesman, rather than feeling "above" him. As the book progresses, Lawrence experiences more and more frequently this journey into the heart of his own savage darkness, feels more and more capable of the brutality of a less-developed people, as we see especially in the massacre of Turks at Tafas in the last book of Seven Pillars. He identifies himself with the Beduin and with outlaw town Arabs, and pays the price for this affinity. He begins to wonder just who he is and what, if anything, in his beliefs separates him from this tough people. It is the same journey Kurtz makes; if Kurtz goes farther, it is because he has no Allenby—and no conscience—to lean on. This is the source of Lawrence's final feeling that he has "prostituted" himself to "Yahoos," when he frees himself from the movement and steps back to take a good look at it and himself in it, still under its influence however. In *Lord Jim*, Conrad—in the voice of Marlow—concludes that without firm faith in the idea of a mission, giving one's life to men of brown, yellow, or black skins "was like selling your soul to a brute" (pp. 338-39), the very phrase Lawrence uses—and Lawrence was a close correspondent of Conrad's and read most of his books. Because of Lawrence's lack of the colonialist's faith and sense of mission, he becomes ultimately a nihilist.

The execution of Hamed (discussed in my third chapter), which he terms "Another Murder" (S, 182) is a way station on Lawrence's pilgrimage into overt violence. A more subtle force operating on him in the same way is the key to the Arab war, preaching, which he terms the "diathetic" element. Instead of merely advising Feisal or leading militarily, Lawrence must continually project himself into the shoes of people fighting for their own national liberation: "the diathetic for us would be more than half the command" (S, 195). The nature of this war itself pushes Lawrence more and more into his Arab role, and by Chapter 36 he speaks of "the mental tug of war" between honesty to the Arabs and loyalty to "my English masters" (S, 213), a phrase which indicates the depth of Lawrence's estrangement from his own people even by this point in the narrative.

As Lawrence slides more deeply into involvement in the Arab movement, his character sketches become more full and subtle; in Chapter 36, he amplifies his view of Abdullah, Feisal's brother. But as Blackmur correctly comments, Lawrence's characters remain "asserted," external rather than internal, outlined rather than portrayed in depth. Either they are dumb like Lynden Bell, heroic like Auda, corrupt like the Bey at Deraa, or "good" like Nasir. But this is because Lawrence wanted to write a broad background for his epic, in which the spotlight shines fully only on his autobiographical self. His characters remain the one or two dimensional creations of a Morris romance rather than the deeply realized studies of a modern novel. Auda, for instance, in contrast with Feisal and Abdullah, appears in Shaw's words as a "Verdi baritone," strong in war and comic in peace. Instead of a fault, this is a natural result of Lawrence's literary aims and his genre of poetic autobiography. But another, more practical reason is responsible for the lack of depth in his characters: Lawrence's uncertain grasp of Arabic, which keeps him from appreciating all the nuances of his Arab characters, and prevents his full absorption into the other culture: "The fluency had a lack of grammar, which made my talk a perpetual adventure for my hearers. Newcomers imagined I must be the native of some unknown illiterate district; a shot-rubbish ground of disjected Arabic parts of speech" (S, 233). Despite this, during the long ride to Akaba, "The long ride in company had made companions of our minds and bodies. The hazardous goal was in our thoughts, day and night; consciously and unconsciously we were training ourselves; reducing our wills to the single purpose which oftenest engrossed these odd moments of talk about an evening fire" (S, 260). Where he once could not eat simple dough cake, he now has no trouble in downing "the boiled, upturned heads, propped on their severed stumps of neck, so that the ears, brown like old leaves, flapped out in the rich surface" (S, 266), parts of the flayed lamb offered him during a tribal feast.

This acclimatization is only the symptom of a deeper absorption in the Arab world that Lawrence suspects when he comments, looking ahead, that "after a successful capture of Akaba I would never again possess myself freely" (S, 276). Lawrence sees always in terms of his own psyche, his own personal difficulties of the moment; he does not fully grasp the patterns of colonial behavior against which he is in rebellion during the revolt, or the process of confrontation with the other culture that he experiences. Conrad understands Lawrence's dilemma with respect to the other culture and states it more clearly than Lawrence himself does in *Seven Pillars*. In his short story, "Outpost of Progress," Conrad writes

But the contact with pure, unmitigated savagery, with primitive nature and primitive man, brings sudden and profound trouble into the heart. To the sentiment of being alone of one's kind, to the clear perception of the loneliness of one's thoughts, one's sensations—to the negation of the habitual, which is safe, there is added the affirmation of the unusual, which is dangerous; a suggestion of things vague, uncontrollable, and repulsive, whose discomposing intrusion excites the imagination and tries the civilised nerves of the foolish and wise alike. (Quoted in Sandison, p. 122).

But Conrad is writing fiction, while Lawrence writes an account more directly analogous to Conrad's own diary of his Congo trip.

On the march to Akaba, Lawrence predicts trouble for himself, but still remains happy, hopeful, able to mock Auda's heroic style, even blow out his own camel's brains and laugh: but increasingly after Akaba he can hold less apart from the Arabs and his Western identity becomes more shaky. He becomes more than a mere adviser, and the factors Conrad enumerates above begin to take a greater toll: "Suffice it that since the march to Akaba I bitterly repented my entaglement in the movement, with a bitterness sufficient to corrode my inactive hours, but insufficient to make me cut myself clear of it. Hence the wobbling of my will, and endless, vapid complainings" (*S*, 552). Even at this point, before the taking of Akaba, Lawrence in the Oxford text wishes for a drastic way out of his confusion of loyalties and cultures: "A bodily wound would have been a grateful vent for my internal perplexities, a mouth through which my troubles might have found relief" (*S*, Oxford text, p. 100). Later, he will hope for death in an air crash (*S*, 545).

In the clash between the epic quality of the revolt, which constitutes the Arab veil of Lawrence's personality, and the political and cultural reality of alienation from it, Lawrence resorts to the same tool that Kinglake did for protection against unpleasantness: irony, directed against himself as well as others. In a conversation about astronomy, Lawrence tells Auda that Westerners "want the world's end . . ." (*S*, 282). Auda, in an unusual display of wit, comments that "if the end of wisdom is to add star to star, our foolishness is pleasing." He undercuts Lawrence's strained desire for the absolute, and Lawrence allows him the last word. It is entirely characteristic of Lawrence that the conclusion of the campaign be undercut by the irony of his self-induced fall from his camel. As he recites an Ernest Dowson poem while waiting to be crushed by the charge of his companions' camels, after having "sailed grandly through the air" as the Kennington portrait shows (*S*, 302–3), we get a picture of the aesthete and intellectual totally out of place in his position and environment. Lawrence rarely allows himself to move into the heroic vein without qualification, and his irony helps him to keep a sense of who he is and what his position really amounts to, if less successfully than Kinglake's.

In the capture of Aba el Lissan, "we were subject for the moment to the physical shame of success, a reaction of victory, when it became clear that nothing was worth doing, and that nothing worthy had been done" (*S*, 307). Similarly, the capture of Akaba results for the absolutist Lawrence who must always strive and never reach, in the manner of all romantics, in a feeling of meaninglessness: "In the blank light of victory we could scarcely identify ourselves. We spoke with surprise, sat emptily, fingered upon our white skirts; doubtful if we could understand or learn whom we were. Others' noise was a dreamlike unreality, a singing in ears drowned deep in water. . . . to-day each man owned his desire so utterly that he was fulfilled in it, and became meaningless" (S, 314). Now Lawrence eats the dust of discontent after having achieved his goal; later, he will seek relief from "the almost insane tension of too-constant striving after an ideal" (S, Oxford text, p. 176). In Cairo, he demands from Clayton not less but more free will: "There was much more I felt inclined to do, and capable of doing:—if he thought I had earned the right to be my own master" (S, 323). Later, he will be "tired to death of free-will" (S, 502), and desire the subservient role of his Arab bodyguard. With the capture of Akaba, Lawrence's troubles are about to begin.

VII   *Beyond Akaba: Books 5–10 (Chapters 55–122)*

As Lawrence proceeds deeper into his contact with the Beduin, he realizes that there is more to their culture than bare renunciation. In the Wadi Rumm, he hears an old man who appears out of nowhere like Wordsworth's leech gatherer say that "The love is from God; and of God; and towards God." This one sentence "seemed to overturn my theories of the Arab nature" (S, 357). In contrast with the barren infertility of Lawrence's nihilism, here is another way out. This is Lawrence's Marabar Caves experience; but where Mrs. Moore learns in the caves that nihilism is the truth of the universe instead of Christianity's doctrine of all-embracing order and love, Lawrence here glimpses love and fertility amid the meaninglessness and confusion. In a telling comment that points to possible mutual influence, E. M. Forster finds in this passage a "lodestar" of compassion, which "may lead us through the psychology of *Seven Pillars* as surely as Damascus led us northward through the geography." (*Abinger Harvest*, p. 169) But instead of Lawrence's conclusion, this incident represents only a momentary stage of his relations with the Arabs. As we will find later, the message of *Seven Pillars* in the end is not "God is love," but "God si love," the same message of jumbled meaninglessness that Mrs. Moore learns. Rather than a realization of the ideal of love between peoples, *Seven Pillars* speaks of the abortive attempt at that ideal. Unlike Forster (and Fielding), who recognize the impasse but can be satisfied with something less than an absolute and do not despair, Lawrence becomes a nihilist.

Lawrence tries to "avoid measuring myself against the pitiless Arab standard," which his momentary vision of love has not overturned, and fails. His experience at Deraa serves as the realization of the depth of his absorption into the Arab culture, his belief (whether objectively justified or not) that he has failed to measure up to that standard and that he is more deeply akin to the Arabs as he sees them than he previously thought he was. On the way to the Yarmuk Bridge, Lawrence is happy: "I felt only that it was very gentle, very comfortable, that the air was happy, and my friends content. . . . There was no thought or care at all. My mind was as near stilled those days as ever in my life" (S, 402). Alone with the Arabs on a mission, Lawrence feels at home, content. Lawrence was "admiring ourselves," referring to himself and the Arabs. Yet, *Seven Pillars* moves according to emotional wave crests and troughs, and so Lawrence immediately notes that "to have generalized and called the Arabs pro-English, would have been a folly. Each stranger made his own poor bed among them" (S, 408).

In preaching to the Serahin, Lawrence strikes exactly the right note for the nomads: "To be of the desert was, as they knew, a doom to wage unending battle with an enemy who was not of the world, nor life, nor anything, but hope itself; and failure seemed God's freedom to mankind. . . . Omnipotence and the Infinite were our two worthiest foemen . . ." (S, 412). This is just one example of the kind of Faustian thinking that Lawrence learned from his reading of *Moby Dick:* this might be Ahab speaking. Lawrence projects himself into Beduin minds by fusing his Western striving for an impossible ideal with the Eastern urge toward renunciation; he loses himself in the speech: "for once my picture-taking memory forgot its trade and only felt the slow humbling of the Serahin . . . and at last their flashing eagerness to ride with us, whatever the bourne." Despite Lawrence's dictum that "to the clear-sighted failure was the only goal," he feels "sick with failure" and (S, 424) when the raid collapses owing to chance clumsiness. Although Lawrence does not always practice what he preaches, he has the ability to momentarily at least merge himself completely with the Arab movement.

Finally, at Deraa, he finds out how like an Arab he has become. Lawrence's torture becomes "the earned wages of rebellion" (S, 13) against his Western self. In order to survive, he must suppress his British identity completely, crying out only in Arabic until he faints (S, 444). We should note here that despite Lawrence's feeling of being "completely broken" by this torture, he successfully hid his true identity, and that his choice of Circassian for a surrogate identity was extremely clever, because the Circassians normally speak their own language rather than Arabic and so Lawrence's bad accent and lack of grammar in Arabic would go unnoticed by the Turks, who also did not normally speak Arabic. Yet despite his fortitude as Achilles, Lawrence as Homer feels that this incident took a great toll on his spirit: "in Deraa that night the citadel of my integrity had been irrevocably lost" (S, 447). Five months later, two members of Lawrence's bodyguard are whipped. One member of the guard, Awad, stands up to the beating, and Lawrence calls it off: "the Zaagi's shrill whip-strokes were too cruel for my taught imagination" (S, 486). But the other member, Mahmas, breaks down and cries. Lawrence comments:

> Arabs did not dissect endurance, their crown of manhood, into material and moral, making allowances for nerves. So Mahmas' crying was called fear, and when loosed, he crept out disgraced into the night to hide.
>   I was sorry for Awad: his hardness put me to shame. (S, 486)

The phrase "crown of manhood" is curiously similar to "citadel of my integrity." What happened to Lawrence at Deraa is that he probably submitted to a personal indignity like rape (as he wrote to Mrs. Shaw) in order to protect his true identity, when he found that he could no longer bear the beating. Thus, the Arab Revolt required him to sell or "prostitute" his physical as well as political integrity in its service: this is the dark underside of victory, the price that had to be paid. Although Lawrence did not give his identity away, he saved it only at the expense of his physical and spiritual purity, and therefore feels that he was not as tough as he should have been in resisting the beating. Awad's hardness puts Lawrence to shame in comparison with his own performance at Deraa, and so he fails the test of the Beduin standard for bearing pain.

At the same time, he realizes how much like an Arab he is. In speaking of his bodyguard, he stresses their attraction to pain: "Pain was to them a solvent, a cathartic, almost a decoration, to be fairly worn when they survived it" (S, 466). In both the Oxford and final texts, Lawrence admits his own discovered masochistic pleasure in pain. In the Oxford text, Lawrence feels that a part of him has "gone dead" as a result of this beating: his Western self has "gone dead" for the moment, but we should note that twenty days later he is standing at Allenby's side in captured Jerusalem, enjoying "the supreme moment of the war" (S, 453), and comments on this in his synopsis, "I find healing in Jerusalem" (S, 13). This is indeed a section of ironies, very bitter ones: the failure at the Yarmuk bridge parallels Lawrence's felt personal failure at Deraa and the result, strangely enough, of all this action of Book 6 is supreme British victory, which is placed significantly on the last page of the book (*S*, 453). Lawrence had to sell out his Western identity in order to help achieve a British victory, and the Deraa incident is the peak, the climax of this drama of the two veils, the place in *Seven Pillars* where Lawrence is forced physically, spiritually, and symbolically to see through the two veils at once. As autobiographer, Lawrence has given us the raw material, but it is the reader who must assemble the pieces to fit this now clear interpretation.

In the very next chapter, Lawrence indirectly and unwittingly connects the effects of the beating with the theme of the cultural dichotomy:

> Now I found myself dividing into parts. There was one which went on riding wisely, sparing or helping every pace of the wearied camel. Another hovering above and to the right bent down curiously, and asked what the flesh was doing. The flesh gave no answer, for, indeed, it was conscious only of a ruling impulse to keep on and on; but a third garrulous one talked and wondered, critical of the body's self-inflicted labour, and contemptuous of the reason for effort. (*S*, 452)

Now, this is exactly the same wording, and the same effect that Lawrence in the first chapter described as the result of seeing through "the veils at once of two customs, two educations, two environments." But Lawrence does not make the overt connection, and leaves it to us to do so.

What Lawrence found out at Deraa is exactly what the alien environment teaches Kurtz. Having been forced to experience brutal actions that would normally have been morally impossible for him as a puritan and Englishman in his usual Oxford environment, Lawrence finds that he likes them to some degree. Like Kurtz, Lawrence learns that he

> lacked restraint in the gratification of his various lusts, and there was something wanting in him—some small matter which, when the pressing need arose, could not be found under his magnificent eloquence. . . . the wilderness found him out early, and had taken on him a terrible vengeance for the fantastic invasion. I think it whispered to him things about himself which he did not know, things of which he had no conception until he took counsel with the great solitude—and the whisper had proved irresistibly fascinating. It echoed loudly with him because he was hollow at the core.

Is it not this hollowness at the core of which Lawrence tells us in the chapter on himself?:

There was a special attraction in beginnings, which drove me into everlasting endeavor to free my personality from accretions and project it on a fresh medium, that my curiosity to see its naked shadow might be fed. The invisible self appeared to be reflected clearest in the still water of another man's yet incurious mind. . . . Much of my doing was from this egoistic curiosity. (S, 566)

Lawrence is a man who defines himself against the outside world. Consequently, when he is with the Arabs, he becomes an Arab; when sipping tea with Dawnay, British—or, to serve his special purposes, he plays the Arab before the British, or the Englishman before the Arabs. The actor gets lost among his roles.

Most of all, he wants to be told what to do and what to be. Hence his attraction to Allenby and earlier, Hogarth:

Always in working I had tried to serve, for the scrutiny of leading was too prominent. Subjection to order achieved economy of thought, the painful, and was a cold-storage for character and Will, leading painlessly to the oblivion of activity. It was part of my failure never to have found a chief to use me. All of them, through incapacity or timidity or liking, allowed me too free a hand; as if they could not see that voluntary slavery was the deep pride of a morbid spirit, and vicarious pain its gladdest decoration. . . .

Feisal was a brave, weak, ignorant spirit, trying to do work for which only a genius, a prophet or a great criminal, was fitted. I served him out of pity, a motive which degraded us both. Allenby came nearest to my longings for a master, but I had to avoid him, not daring to bow down for fear lest he show feet of clay with that friendly word which must shatter my allegiance. Yet, what an idol the man was to us. . . . (S, 565)

The Oxford text makes this desire for outside control even more clear. In sum, "the truth was I did not like the 'myself' I could see and hear" (S, 566). Colin Wilson (in The Outsider, Boston, 1956) characterizes this type of man and particularly Lawrence as "the Outsider," one who cannot find his real self and can only desire control from the outside as a substitute. Lawrence's ease in changing names, dropping identities, especially in connection with his surrendering to the slavery of the ranks in The Mint, corroborates this view of him.

Much like Kurtz, who "could get himself to believe anything— anything" (Heart of Darkness, p. 65) and ends by believing in nothing, Lawrence finds that "The practice of our revolt fortified the nihilist attitude in me" (S, 468). Like a piece of pliable metal, Lawrence is bent back and forth between his two cultures until he snaps. He has no clear-cut self to oppose to this fluctuating motion. After Deraa, Lawrence does not care a "hoot" (S, 447) about the Arab movement, he says, and after Zeid spends foolishly the all-important gold, Lawrence decides to follow through in the hollow spirit of a games-player: "It might be fraud or it might be farce: no one should say that I could not play it" (S, 503). Also, "My will had gone and I feared to be alone, lest the winds of circumstance, or power, or lust, blow my empty soul away" (S, 502). Lawrence has in his own eyes failed in the test of will at Deraa, and learned unpleasant things about himself, but his saving grace, the thing that prevents total abandonment *à la* Kurtz, is this sense of puritanical conscience, the fear of his soul being "blown away."

In the last two books of *Seven Pillars,* the drama of the two veils reaches its culmination: owing to the combined participation of English and Arab troops, Lawrence sees the two cultures side by side. The fluctuations build to a crescendo: "In my English capacity I shared this view, but on my Arab side both agitation and battle seemed equally important, the one to serve the joint success, the other to establish Arab self-respect, without which victory would not be wholesome" (S, 539). Even his aesthetic perceptions have changed, owing to his immersion in the Arab culture: "For the rest they were a broad-faced, low-browed people, blunt-featured beside the fine-drawn Arabs whom generations of in-breeding had sharpened to a radiance ages older than the primitive, blotched, honest Englishmen. Continental soldiers looked lumpish beside our lean-bred fellows: but against my supple Nejdis the British in their turn looked lumpish" (S, 544). The Continentals come out lowest in this scale, but "*my* supple Nejdis" top the British in beauty. At the same moment that he calls the Arabs "*my,*" he refers to the British soldiers as "*our* lean-bred fellows," a small symptom of the cultural dichotomy in Lawrence's mind. Now he tries to identify with England, the power for which he has traded "the citadel of my integrity": "We English, who lived years abroad among strangers, went always dressed in the pride of our remembered country, that strange entity which had no part with the inhabitants. . ." (S, 544). Memmi notices a common characteristic of colonialists: "Having assigned to his homeland the burden of his own decaying grandeur, he expects it to respond to his hopes. He wants it to merit his confidence, to reflect on him the image of itself which he desires. . . . Often, by dint of hoping he ends up beginning to believe it." (Memmi, p. 59). Lawrence lacks even this consolation. In the Oxford text, he comments at this point that "We idealised our country so highly, that when we returned sometimes the reality fell too short of our dreams to be tolerable" (S, Oxford text, p. 228).

A simple but telling illustration of Lawrence's position between the veils occurs on pages 568–69. Although "our Imperial Camel Corps" is a great British institution, Lawrence, riding Arab style with his bodyguard, "would gain three miles on the British" and watch the Camel Corps come up. Lawrence tells his guard that he could find forty men among the British who would "out-ride, out-fight, and out-suffer any forty men in Feisal's army." Yet, on the same page two paragraphs later, Lawrence's own guard appear as "the best camel-masters for hire in Arabia." A detail perhaps, but such details occur frequently and point to a deeper meaning.

The fluctuations become more rapid and disordered:

. . . on this march to Damascus (and such it was already in my imagination) my normal balance had changed. I could feel the taut power of Arab excitement behind me. The climax of the preaching of years had come, and a united country was straining toward its historic capital. In confidence that this weapon, tempered by myself, was enough for the utmost of my purpose, I seemed to forget the English companions who stood outside my idea in the shadow of ordinary war. I failed to make them partners of my certainty. (S, 583)

In the midst of this completeness of the Arab veil, Lawrence's British self slips back into place unexpectedly when he sees the two armies side by side at Azrak:

. . . the wind in the dusty green branches played with such sounds as it made in English trees. It told me I was tired to death of these Arabs; petty incarnate Semites who attained heights and depths beyond our reach, though not beyond our sight. They realized our absolute in their unrestrained capacity for good and evil; and for two years I had profitably shammed to be their companion. (S, 586)

Rather than a hypocritical glorification of or attack on one side or the other, Lawrence gives us here the tortured confusion through which he lived in the form of contradictory passages not more than three pages apart. Sometimes he stands apart from both sides, and views them from a distance: "It was a thing typical, as instinct with our national character as the babbling laughing turmoil over there was Arab. In their crises the one race drew in, the other spread" (*S*, 589). Here "our" is British, although Lawrence clinically dissects both British and Arabs. In the Oxford text at this point, "ourselves" sets Lawrence against the British: "I was accustomed, callous now, to the Arab courage, for they were fighting for their freedom, a very urgent end, but these English were men as good as ourselves, but moved only by duty, or the mass-instinct of industry" (*S*, Oxford text, p. 262). Later Lawrence is "jealous for the Arab honour, in whose service I would go forward at all costs" (*S*, 624).

A peak of involvement in his Arab veil comes for Lawrence at the village of Tafas in Chapter 118. Back near Deraa ten months after his own torture there, Lawrence catalogs the Turkish atrocities against the villagers of Tafas as a doubling of his own sufferings: "I looked close and saw the body of a woman folded across it, bottom upwards, nailed there by a saw bayonet whose haft stuck hideously into the air from between her naked legs. She had been pregnant, and about her lay others, perhaps twenty in all, variously killed, but set out in accord with an obscene taste" (*S*, 631). The catalog of atrocities is meant to justify the fact that "By my order we took no prisoners, for the only time in our war" (*S*, 632), for "In a madness born of the horror of Tafas we killed and killed, even blowing in the heads of the fallen and of the animals; as though their death and running blood could slake our agony" (*S*, 633). Though couched in a Homeric tone of justified revenge, including Tallal's brave charge, it is clear that here as in the killing of Hamed and the massacre at Wadi Hesa "There was no glory left, but the terror of the broken flesh" (*S*, 482). In these events, full of the barbarism of primitive war, Lawrence's imitation of the natives has gone beyond an act, and like Kurtz, he has realized an "unrestrained capacity" for evil in himself.

Lawrence begins to waken fully from the dream of the last two years as he nears Damascus, and finds himself "strangely alone" (*S*, 641). In a passage of deep sensual perception, he realizes his total alienation from both sides:

About the soldiers hung the Arabs: gravely gazing men from another sphere. My crooked duty had banished me among them for two years. To-night I was nearer to them than to the troops, and I resented it, as shameful. The intruding contrast mixed with longing for home, to sharpen my faculties and make fertile my distaste, till not merely did I see the unlikeness of race, and hear the unlikeness of language, but I learned to pick between their smells: the heavy, standing, curdled sourness of dried sweat in cotton, over the Arab crowds; and the feral smell of English soldiers: that hot pissy aura of thronged men in woollen clothes: a tart pungency, breathcatching, ammoniacal; a fervent fermenting naptha smell. (S, 642)

His duty completed at great physical and mental price to himself, his absolute still unrealized, his position between colonizer and colonized more sharply defined than ever, Lawrence finds that his new loneliness makes final victory "sorrowful" and the phrase of freedom "meaningless" (S, 652). Wading through the filth of the Turkish barracks in his white robes, Lawrence feels that "anyone who pushed through to success a rebellion of the weak against their masters must come out of it so stained in estimation that nothing in the world would make him feel clean" (S, 659). Victory has cost him the loss of integrity involved in a glimpse into his own heart of darkness: "God si love." Lawrence's best efforts, carried through at so much cost to himself, as in cleaning out the Turkish hospital, earn only a slap in the face. Rarely has an idealistic dreamer been forced down to earth so harshly.

It is not hard to see why a reading of Lawrence's book helped Forster finish his own *A Passage to India*, as he wrote to T. E. in February, 1924: "By the way your book helped me to finish a book of my own. Seemed to pull me together." (*Letters to T. E.*, p. 62). It is even less of a wonder that Lawrence saw his own situation mirrored in the pages of Forster's book:

If excellence of materials meant anything, my book would be as good as yours: but it stinks of me: whereas yours is universal: the bitter terrible hopeless picture a cloud might have painted, of man in India. You surpass the Englishman and surpass the Indian, and are neither: and yet there is nothing inhuman (like Moby Dick) in your picture. . . .
If the flea may assert a kindred feeling with the lion . . . then let me suggest how my experience (and abandonment) of work in Arabia repeats your history of a situation-with-no-honest-way-out-of-it. You on the large thinking plane, me on the cluttered plane of action . . . and both lost. (*L*, 462).

What Lawrence has learned in Arabia is exactly what Mrs. Moore learned in India: "Pathos, piety, courage—they exist, but are identical, and so is filth. Everything exists, nothing has value." His experience in Arabia results in "a muddle (as we call it), a frustration of reason and form."

In ending in a muddle of identity, Lawrence exemplifies the plight of all the British colonial characters of the early twentieth century who go wrong, as portrayed in the literature of the period:

In Kipling the struggle for mastery is evident in every story which has to deal with the country, and nine times out of ten, "great, grey, formless India" wins. Inevitably it comes to represent the forces of persecution ranged against the individual in his struggle to sustain his own identity. Physically and morally it overwhelms and crushes. One's own truths and moral definitions blur and diffuse themselves into meaninglessness, just as they did for Forster's Mrs. Moore. Mrs. Mallowe has, in fact, occasional flashes of Mrs. Moore's perception, observing very clearly the moral destructiveness of India where "you can't focus anything." (Sandison, p. 79).

Like all the colonial heroes—and war heroes—of this period who learned too much, Lawrence returns home unable to "focus anything." He has learned that true friendship between alien peoples is impossible: in Forster's words, "alas, the two nations cannot be friends." (*Passage to India*, p. 311). He has learned unpleasant truths about himself and his own dark corners of savagery and masochism. If there is any fitting message of *Seven Pillars*, it is Kurtz' "The horror! The horror!"

CHAPTER 6

Seven Pillars of Wisdom: *Literary Evaluation*

I N the act of assessing any autobiography as a literary form, the critic must always bear in mind that he is not dealing with fiction, but with a different genre which operates according to its own principles. A failure to understand this fact has distorted the judgments of previous critics of *Seven Pillars* (and *The Mint*); and in fact it is only recently, with our new scientific understanding of the autobiography, that we can arrive at a definitive evaluation. The differences between an autobiography and a novel appear in the source, or the artist and his intention; in the form, or the techniques which embody the artist's intention; and in the end, the effect that the work has on its audience. The following model gives in schematic form the particular elements that any critic of autobiography must consider.

Model of Autobiography

Source (Artist)

1. Artist's intention.
2. Artist's situation at the time of writing.
3. The artist as narrator and protagonist.
4. Actual internal and external events of the artist's life.

Form (Technique)

1. Shape or Structure.
   A. Temporal shape: the selection of events.
   B. Spatial shape: the arrangement of events.
      a. Chronological series.
      b. Disjunction.
      c. Journey. (Protagonist's personality and life grows outward or inward).
      d. Conversion. (Action builds up to and away from a particular event).

   C. Ideological shape: the interpretation and patterns the narrator sees in
       events; the relationship between inner and outer events that he
       presents.
   D. Literary parallel or model: the picaresque novel, the comic epic, the
       oration, the sermon, the history, etc.
2. Characterization: internal or external view, static or dynamic growth,
    smooth or disjunct presentation of the development of narrator, pro-
    tagonist and other characters.
3. Style: narrator's tool of interpretation and expression.
   A. Detachment or involvement.
   B. Central metaphors and imagery.
   C. Rhetorical or organic, conscious or unselfconscious.

End (Effect on audience)
1. Truth or sincerity: reader's expectation and judgment.
2. Projection of artist's personality. Does the reader feel that he knows what
    it is like to be the artist?

Depending on the particular subgenre of autobiography (oratorical,
dramatic, or poetic) under consideration, the various elements of
source and form will receive different weight: for instance, the poetic
autobiographer almost invariably fails to place an ideological shape on
his personality, while the oratorical autobiographer, in his role as
narrator, almost always does, continually telling us what to think and
what his intention is; the dramatic autobiographer writes an unselfconscious, picaresque kind of work, with style to match, and the
oratorical autobiographer chooses a high, rhetorical, sermonlike
style. But no matter how source and form may differ according to
subgenre, the end of all types or subgenres of autobiography remains
the same: to project the personality of the writer. In a novel, we judge
the author for his ability to sublimate his own personality in the
personalities of his characters; in autobiography, we judge him for his
ability to project his own personality. Truly, the one final question
that we ask about every autobiography is, do we know what it is like to
be the author after having read it? If the answer is yes, the autobiography is successful as a literary work.
   When we ask this question of *Seven Pillars,* our answer is an
undoubted affirmative. Lawrence's intentions may have been divided when he wrote it; he may not be able to explain his personality
fully or why he acted as he did; but there is no doubt that he transmits
to the reader his own sense of internal fragmentation, of being split
open by the events of the revolt. We know what it felt like to be T. E.

Lawrence during the course of the revolt, harrowing as that knowledge is, and must judge *Seven Pillars* a highly successful autobiography as a result.

In previous chapters of this book, we have already discussed several of the elements of autobiographical source, form, and end. Under the heading of source, we saw that Lawrence's intention was split and uncertain. In the first chapter of the Oxford text, he writes that ". . .the book is a designed procession of Arab freedom from Mecca to Damascus. It was intended to rationalise the campaign, that everyone might see how natural the success was, and how inevitable, how little dependent on direction or brain, how much less on the outside assistance of the few British. . . .In these pages is not the history of the Arab movement, but just the story of what happened to me in it." And we saw that despite this divided intention, *Seven Pillars* is really an autobiography that presents the development of Lawrence's personality in relation to the external events of the revolt (however thinly the connection is made), rather than a history or memoir of the revolt alone. We also demonstrated Lawrence's situation at the time of writing, that he was still too close to events to distance himself from them, and as a result presents us with the raw materials of a process rather than an interpretation of that process; and that he unites narrator and protagonist in one "I." The final result of all this is that, under form, it is the reader who must impose the shape on Lawrence's personality, who must create Lawrence in the image of other characters in the early twentieth-century literature of British imperialism. But we stated quite clearly that this necessity to create a coherent personality of the protagonist is an interesting burden laid on all readers of poetic autobiography, a normal characteristic of the genre, and not a literary flaw. Under end, we discussed the truth content of Lawrence's autobiography and decided that he gives in *Seven Pillars* despite some variations according to text, an essentially true and sincere account of his view of the Arab Revolt and his part in it. Now we must look at the remaining elements in the model in order to determine precisely *how* Lawrence managed to succeed in projecting his personality.

I *Temporal and Spatial Shape*

As Lawrence himself and the critics have long known, *Seven Pillars* contains two plot lines: the first, which provides the basic framework and backbone of the book, is the military action which culminates in victory in Damascus; the second is the bitter personal story of

Lawrence's trading "the citadel of my integrity" for that military victory. In this section, we will analyze the main structural or shaping principle of both plot lines, and show how they are sometimes counterpointed with great effect.

In the chapter on "Strangeness and Pain," Lawrence writes that "we lived always in the stretch or sag of nerves, either on the crest or in the trough of waves of feeling" (*S*, 29). Both plot lines are organized in terms of wave crests and troughs. In the personal plot, Lawrence is either ecstatic about the possibility of reaching a distant goal, or depressed after reaching it; either a full participant in the romantic and heroic hopes of the Arabs, or alienated from them, a British agent. But his ups and downs are not explained always with reference to external events, and this plot line appears chaotic as a result, especially toward the end of the book, when his shifts between the veils occur on almost every page. The military plot, which roughly follows the outlines of the campaign from start to finish, is by contrast much more highly and successfully organized, and its waves and troughs are congruent with simple military success or failure. Let us look at Lawrence's means of shaping this military plot.

The title, "Seven Pillars of Wisdom," which can be explicated in so many ways, either as in my last chapter, or as a reference to Ruskin's "Seven Lamps of Architecture" (as O'Donnell and Meyers point out), or as a reference to the seven biblical lands which must be governed morally,[1] refers first and foremost to the military architecture of the revolt. A manuscript notebook (MS. Eng 1252, 355) in the Houghton Library makes this clear and demonstrates the fundamental importance of the military plot to Lawrence's conception of the book's structure.

In that notebook, we find that Lawrence first envisioned *Seven Pillars* as comprising eight books, each of which is comparable to the states of building a house of military knowledge. Thus, Book 1 ("To the end of Arab Bureau and my going down") is labeled "Materials"; Book 2, ("Jidda, Rabegh, Feisal and Khartoum"), "Foundations"; Book 3 ("Yenbo, Nakhl Mubarak and Wejh"), "First Courses"; Book 4 ("Wadi Ais, Rly., Art of War"), "Scaffolding"; Book 5 ("Akaba, Blowing of Trains, Preaching"), "Pillars"; Book 6 ("Bridges and Winter War"), "Faults"; Book 7 ("Amman, Maan, Shawm Hesa"), "Reconstruction"; and Book 8 ("Plain and safeguards and Azrak Deraa Damascus"), "House is Perfected." These stages refer to the military building of the revolt, rather than to Lawrence's personal struggle, which can scarcely be so neatly schematized. The phrase "seven pillars of wisdom," according to this scheme, refers to the strength of the consolidated military knowledge necessary to the construction of a successful revolt.

A clear reference to this meaning of the title and to the basically military conception of the book remains embedded in the final text:

When it grew too hot for dreamless dozing, I picked up my tangle again, and went on ravelling it out, considering now the whole house of war in its structural aspect, which was strategy, in its arrangements, which were tactics, and in the sentiment of its inhabitants, which was psychology; for my personal duty was command, and the commander, like the master architect, was responsible for all. (S, 191—92.)

Lawrence, attempting to be a "master architect" of war and literature, strives for the kind of comprehensive literary framework for his personality that Doughty, for instance, was unable to attain.

Although to his critics the military plot takes a subordinate place to the story of personal doubt and failure—as well it should—this basic plot remains interesting and exciting not only for its content, but for the usually romantic style of narration. The basic plot contains—in addition to antiromantic and antiheroic tales of failures, ignobility, and massacres—Lawrence's grab at glorious adventures properly belonging to centuries previous to his, and ours, while the introspective process is pure twentieth century in its movement toward final fragmentation and dislocation. Lawrence fits a modern mentality into a narrative of romance by counterpointing military ups with personal downs and thus creating the mixed mood that prevails throughout the book, especially after Akaba. Thus, as we have already noticed, the capture of Akaba, glorious as it is, results in a sense of personal worthlessness and worry for Lawrence. The failure at the Yarmuk bridges and the personal failure at Deraa are purposely counterpointed against Lawrence's appearance in Jerusalem as military victor, at Allenby's side, occurring as all these events do in Book 6. And of course the final victory at Damascus only means personal alienation for Lawrence, as the filthy Turkish barracks are deliberately contrasted with his white robes and the victory celebrations outside. Sometimes we may not understand just why Lawrence feels so worthless when events would make a normal person feel just the opposite, but when this counterpoint works, as it does in Book 6 and at the end of *Seven Pillars*, the effect is grating and powerful, a statement of the death-in-life caused by World War I. We may not understand fully why victory at Akaba makes Lawrence feel meaningless, but we do finally understand why the ultimate victory leaves him a hollow shell, even if we forget our external knowledge of the S. A. story and simply base our feeling on what is contained between the two covers of the book.

In the shaping of the military plot line, Lawrence is successful in conveying the external drama of the adventure in a consistently engrossing manner far surpassing the interest of the normal memoir. In the military campaign, success at Akaba is followed by failure at the Yarmuk bridge, a period of regrouping of energies, and a final victorious sweep. The drama here is that of the novice at war who gradually perfects his abilities as a commander through trial and error and leads a national movement to overcome its oppressors. We watch Lawrence's experiments as he gains a confident control of the materials of command. "War was made up of crises of intense effort" (*S*, 511), and we move from peaks of excitement to troughs of inactivity in a calculated course. Lawrence demonstrates in the letters his concern over structuring this movement of the book from action to speculation and rest to renewed action, the wave which finally breaks over Damascus. To Forster, he writes that he "let the activity of the book fall into a trough for twenty pages, to give my imaginary reader a rest before piling up the agony of the last advance on Damascus" (*L*, 457). To Garnett, he expresses the fear that the last fifty pages are "flatter than the VIth and VIIth parts (the failure of the bridge and the winter war) and formed an anticlimax—a weak ending" (*L*, 368).

In the structuring of the war narrative, Lawrence accomplishes his goal of presenting architecturally the difficulty of consolidating the house of military wisdom and action. He conveys the feeling of retrogression and advance that he experienced as the commander of the revolt. Within each book, we have the effect of traveling from peak to trough to peak that see in the larger military structure of *Seven Pillars*. For instance, within Book 7 itself, Lawrence's exhiliration at Tafileh gives way to despair when he learns that Zeid has squandered the gold. On the larger level, the failure of the Yarmuk bridge (in which Lawrence is personally involved, unlike the capture of Jerusalem which is noted in the same book) in Book 6 follows the "flat" period of minor raids of Book 5 which in its turn follows the high peak of the capture of Akaba in Book 4. Here are two long marches which produce opposite results, separated by a "flat": two wave crests of emotion, one positive and one negative, with a trough in between.

Although Lawrence's book follows a chronological diary sequence, some days take pages to recount, while others are passed over in silence or in a few paragraphs, as Robert Payne points out. By means of these selective stresses, Lawrence shapes the drama. Events too "flat," like the abortive reconaissance raid of the Oxford text which disappears from Book 8 of the final edition, are eliminated. Lawrence keeps us balancing between the peaks and troughs of dramatic emotion by making rigorous use of the autobiographer's technique of dwelling on the most interesting events. In war as in art, Lawrence—far from being a nihilist—struggles to impose a coherent pattern on his materials. His personal tragedy is that because of the essential hollowness of his own character, intellectual control failed him when he needed it most in life, and the personal sections of *Seven Pillars* reflect this fact. Only in *The Mint* is he redeemed. If the shape of the military plot is a chronological series, the personal plot is a longer inner journey.

II *Characterization*

As already stated, where we would judge a novelist by his ability to project himself into the many roles and minds of his characters, we expect the author of an autobiography to project his own personality and to place the mark of that personality on all characters and events in his book. Lawrence recognized clearly this aspect of autobiography: "Doughty's book mirrored Doughty as much as it mirrored Arabia." (*Men in Print*, p. 43). We want to open an autobiography to any page and sense the author's personality infusing every sentence on that page, every event, and every character.

A failure to understand the nature of the genre of poetic autobiography in which Lawrence is writing leads R. P. Blackmur to tack a mistaken conclusion on an otherwise highly perceptive analysis of *Seven Pillars:* "When we say that Lawrence never produced a character, not even his own, if we add that he produced nevertheless almost everything that makes for character, we have said very nearly what is necessary. It was his everlasting effort." (Blackmur, p. 123). As we have stated earlier, the creation of the protagonist's character is a task which the reader of Lawrence's book—and all poetic autobiographies—must perform, based on the raw materials given him by the author. Lawrence gives us "everything that makes for" his own character, and we have to shape it ourselves. By the same token, the other characters in the book are seen through the eyes of the author and reflect, not objective truth or the actual inner working of their own minds, but only the impression they made on the author. They become aspects of *his* personality, they are fit into the pattern of *his* sensibility, and cannot be the deeply realized characters of a modern novel who stand on their own feet, or photographically true images of the real figures on which they are based. In other words, as these characters appear in *Seven Pillars,* they reflect only those aspects of the real figures that struck Lawrence, and which he thought they should reflect. Thus, he refused to change his depictions of Hubert Young and Meinertzhagen despite protests by both that his portraits were not mirror images of themselves. In *Seven Pillars,* Meinertzhagen appears as an archsadist who enjoyed "spattering the brains of a cornered mob of Germans one by one with his African knob-kerri" (*S,* 384). About this, Meinertzhagen states in his *Middle East Diary, 1917–1956* (London, 1959, pp. 31–32) that ". . . I told him I had been considering what he said about me in his book and begged him to expunge it as the first part was not true and put me in a false light. Then he started. He surprised me by saying that little of his book was strict truth, though most of it was based on fact. . . ." In making this "admission," Lawrence simply certified that he was an autobiographer rather than a historian. He did not want to understand Young or Meinertzhagen in depth; what he wanted was to fit them into the pattern of his own sensibility, and that sensibility is best served by extravagant descriptions and rich images. A mild Meinertzhagen probably never appeared to Lawrence's eyes, and would not do against a background of striking and sharply etched characters.

As Blackmur points out, "To put it unkindly, his Arabs, and his English, and himself, too, all play character parts, they all work on formulas, however unpredictable and unusual; but, to make it praise, the formulas are intensely felt and the working out all fits into the game recorded." (Blackmur, p. 104). Auda may or may not have been an innocent, heroic child; but the modern Lawrence saw him as such and remembered him as such when it came to writing *Seven Pillars.* As he tells us himself, his diary was not full of objective descriptions of places and events, but rather this reactions to them. Like Kinglake, Lawrence "dwells precisely upon those matters which happened to interest me, and upon no others," (*Eothen,* p. xvii), and that goes for characters as well as events. Like the Beduin in general, all the characters in the book are created to one degree or another in Lawrence's own image.

Because Lawrence's image includes a mind full of Homeric and chivalric impressions, his characters scarcely lack color and interest. As Blackmur says, "the formulas are intensely felt." We do not easily forget Feisal as he appears in Lawrence's introductory picture. He is not allowed to perform enough and in varied enough situations to permit us to form our own assessment of him, free of the author's assertions about his worth or lack of it; as Forster remarked, "All your characters tend to go *quiet* when the eye is removed. . . ." (*Letters to T. E.*, p. 59). But when our eye is on the characters, they are very colorful indeed, and even Lawrence's assertions about them are always powerfully stated and affecting. In the end, the question of Lawrence's projection of his own personality and that of others hinges entirely on the most important technical element in any literary work: its style.

III   *Lawrence's Stylistic Aesthetic*

If style—the right word in the right place, according to Coleridge—is important in fiction, it is particularly and even more so in poetic autobiography, where the author's *primary* concern is not the presentation of an exciting plot or the depth psychology of a group of characters, but the forceful exposition of his own personality, which he does not fully understand. The poetic autobiographer reveals himself to the reader most clearly not by recording inner and outer events, the significance of which he does not always fully grasp himself, but through his manner of expressing himself. This manner clues us in as it were on what he really thinks about the events he describes, and hence on who he is. And in fact poetic autobiographers, like Thoreau, Whitman, Yeats, and James (to name only a few), are all masters of style.

As R. P. Blackmur correctly noticed, the true unity of Lawrence's *Seven Pillars* lies not in the military framework, which only superficially holds the book together, but in Lawrence's own sensibility, those elements of his personality which make Lawrence who he is and not someone else: "Wholeness, for Lawrence, lay in the sensibility; so far as its elements could be expressed, they would make a unity that might be taken as complete if taken at all: the unity of obsession" (Blackmur, pp. 106-07). In a letter to Ede of December 25, 1928, Lawrence expressed his very conscious realization of the use of style to express his personality:

I find that my fifth writing (after perhaps fifteenth reading) of a sentence makes it more shapely, pithier, stranger than it was. Without that twist of strangeness no one would feel an individuality, a differentness, behind the phrase. Unless it stays long enough in your thinking box to catch your likeness, it will not be demonstrably yours: and if anybody else could have written it, then it's no good. (*Letters to Ede*, p. 27).

Lawrence's feeling of the necessity for every sentence to be his grows naturally out of the literary philosophy of his masters, Pater, Ruskin, Doughty, and Morris. For them, even descriptive or analytical essays on scientific topics would have to be written in highly individual styles, by means of which the reader could instantly recognize who the writer was (as Doughty's refusal to revise his difficult English for the benefit of the Royal Geographical Society proves). Today, authors of essays and reports strive to write a clear, objective prose in which their own personalities cannot be recognized and which readers cannot recognize as the work of a particular author. Written as it was in the 1920s, when the period of personalized prose was already past, *Seven Pillars* appeared as a throwback in style as well as heroic content, and found its greatest acceptance among older writers, like H. G. Wells and Arnold Bennett, who were able to appreciate its virtues independently of current fashions. Thus, Wells is reliably reported to have referred to Lawrence's book as "the finest piece of prose that has been written in the English language for 150 years." (*T. E. by Friends*, p. 131). Arnold Bennett compares T. E. favorably to D. H. Lawrence, and finds T. E. "a better writer than Winston Churchill. He is one of the best English prose writers living, but . . . doesn't always know when to stop. He thinks in separate words. Seemingly he has passed unscathed through a world bristling with clichés." (Houghton Library MS Eng. 1252, 362). And John Buchan, the author of the thriller *The Thirty-Nine Steps*, wrote Lawrence that "When you do not get inundated with adjectives you are the best living writer of English prose" (*Letters to T. E.*, p. 21). In the end, Lawrence based his own assessment of *Seven Pillars* on its style: "However, granted that the *Seven Pillars* is not wholly contemptible, as prose. I can concede that much, I think" (*L*, 586).

Although Lawrence's letters reveal a concern with the temporal and spatial shape of his book, as we have seen, his most interesting and detailed comments relate to the art of style. His method of styling his work was first to write down his sentences quickly and spontaneously, as we see in his claim that Book 6 "was written entire between sunrise and sunset" (*S*, 21) and that ninety-five percent of Text II was written in thirty days. Then he would return over the sentences again and again, making sure that each captured his individuality. So Lawrence's style has both a romantic spontaneity, a very deep expression of his feelings at the moment of writing, *and* a very deliberate and conscious polish. Lawrence indicates this balance between spontaneity and polish not only in the Ede letter quoted above, but in a longer statement to Vyvyan Richards, which also clarifies his stylistic intentions:

. . . prose depends on a music in one's head which involuntarily chooses & balances the possible words to *keep tune* with the thought. The best passages in English prose all deal with death or the vanity of things, since that is a tune we all know, and the mind is set quite free to think while writing about it. Only it can't be kept up very long, because of the mortal weakness and the wear and tear of things, & the function of criticism, revision & correction (polishing) seems to me to be either
    (i) *putting* a thing into thought
    (ii) [putting] thought into rhythm
    (iii) putting expression into meaning
It seems to me that if you think too hard about the form, you forget the matter, & if your brain is wrestling with the matter, you may not have attention to spare for the manner. Only occasionally in things constantly dwelt upon, do you get an unconscious balance, & then you get a *spontaneous* and perfect arrangement of words to fit the idea, *as the tune*. Polishing is an attempt, by stages, to get to what should be a single combined stride. (*L*, 318)

Thus, Lawrence works toward a perfect matching of form and content, expression and subject, which should appear spontaneous. In his choice of a musical analogy for style, he reveals his debt to late nineteenth-century critical theory, in which this analogy is always employed.

In fact, the result of Lawrence's polishing is highly complex, sophisticated, artificial (in the sense of being unlike normal speech) prose rather than a Mozart-like purity and simplicity and clarity. Although Lawrence felt that "Simplicity is as often the mark of a first-class work as complexity is of second-class work" (*Men in Print*, p. 43), he also felt that "so spiced and tormented a generation as ours can hardly be expected to find a simplicity which does not ring false: so perhaps it is better to admit our complexity, and develop it to the nth" (*Men in Print*, pp. 52–53), that his own complex style grew naturally out of his own personality and experiences and thus suited the post–World War I age even as it appeared to be a throwback to the nineteenth century.

In the end, Lawrence approves stylistic complexity and artificiality. One should not play at appearing simple if one has complicated things to say: " . . . I'm sorry for the sophisticated simplicity. That's decadence. If a man is not simple by nature he cannot be simple by art, and if he tries he only achieves a falseness. You can only (if complex) get simplicity by my 'third degree': by distilling a scene into quintessential action" (*L*, 377). Therefore, *Seven Pillars* is "too elaborate and conscious a construction to admit simplicity—or rather, if I were limpid or direct anywhere people would (should) feel a false stillness" (*L*, 371). Lawrence chooses a complicated style to reflect his own complicated personality.

Lawrence's complaint about the style of both Homer and Doughty is that they try for "sophisticated simplicity," a false effect of primitivism. About Homer, he writes in his translator's preface that "Wardour-Street Greek like the *Odyssey's* defies honest rendering . . . the tight lips of archaic art have grown the fixed grin of archaism." Doughty's book suffers from the same fault: "This inlay of strange words into a ground-work of daily English is a mistake. The effect is fussy, not primitive, more peasant art than peasant." Yet when Lawrence describes not himself but Auda, Feisal, Tallal, and Nasir for instance, the same "sophisticated simplicity" that he learned from Homer, Doughty, and Morris and which became a part of his own vision of the world, as we have seen, comes out in chivalric parallel phrases and inversions: " 'What is upon you, Tafas?' said I" (*S*, 82); "the splendid leader, the fine horseman, the courteous and strong companion of the road" (*S*, 633). Yet, despite Lawrence's condemnation of similar effects in Doughty and Homer, we should notice that this style of "sophisticated simplicity" of the Arab portraits in Lawrence as in Doughty is anything but simple to achieve; it is a conscious, artificial, complex effect.

Even if Lawrence is always complex, even when appearing simple, the alert reader notices that *Seven Pillars* is written in more than one style, as Forster points out:

Book being lengthy, you have rightly several styles, one for R. E 8s [airplanes], and that sort of thing, another for normal narrative, another for reflections, another for crises of emotion or beauty. The criticism I'd offer is that your reflective style is not properly under control. Almost at once, when you describe your thoughts, you become obscure, and the slightly strained sense which then (not habitually) you lend words, does not bring your sentence the richness you intended, imparts not colour but gumminess. (*Letters to T. E.*, p. 60).

In this fact of many styles, as in the fact of the two plot lines of the book, we have the key to the confusion of the critics that we noted in Chapter 1 of this study. Some critics stress the adventure story, and thus see the book as highly structured; others, following without understanding the story of the two veils, see only fluctuating confusion. Some critics stress the "limpid" style of the narrative sections, while others decry Lawrence's style as involved or muddy because they emphasize the "gummy" reflective style. The end to this confusion lies in the realization that *Seven Pillars* is a whole poetic autobiography which follows the principles of its genre.

The thing that all Lawrence's styles in *Seven Pillars* have in common is a high-powered complexity, the response Lawrence found most suitable for his own personality and the age, and which reminds us of his love for powerful motorcycle, motorboat, and airplane engines. The whole of the "Strangeness and Pain" chapter is written in a prose influenced by the throb of airplane engines, as Lawrence tells us himself.[2] Yet its total effect remains esoteric, Eastern as well as Western, and not of the modern age. Describing "English Prose between 1919 and 1939" in his *Two Cheers for Democracy*, Forster notes that "The best work of the period has this esoteric tendency. T. E. Lawrence, though heroic in action, retreats into the desert to act" (p. 291). In literature, Lawrence retreated into the exotic land of an art-prose all his own. His concern with alliteration and assonance, with the rise and fall of his paragraphs, with keeping in tune with his subject matter, appears more in line with the poetry of Keats and Swinburne and the prose of Sir Thomas Browne and Thomas Traherne than with the art of his own century. As Forster remarks, *"The Seven Pillars* for all its greatness is too strange a book to be typical of a period . . ." (*Two Cheers*, p. 287). That Lawrence is extremely sensitive to style and aware of the great prose tradition is clear from the several pages of minute stylistic criticism that he wrote on Henry Williamson's *Tarka the Otter*, among which this remark appears: "almost fit, for its wonder, to be put next to Traherne's 'orient wheat,' as one of the finest passages of English prose" (*Men in Print*, p. 48). Vyvyan Richards informs us that "Lawrence himself observed that his paragraphs seemed to rise and rise in a climax and then descend to their finish; and that the culminating point of the climax was commonly marked by the word 'all.' He constantly so analyzed his work as he went along" (Richards, p. 186).

We have proof that Lawrence was aware of the straining of his prose after effects of all kinds. Sometimes, he is unkind to himself in his assessment of this technique: "I wrote this thing in the war atmosphere, and believe that it is stinking with it. Also there is a good deal of cruelty, and some excitement. All these things, in a beginner's hands, tend to force him over the edge, and I suspect there is much over-writing" (*L*, 362). Sometimes, he justifies it: "*The purple passages even when they are meant to be purple.* I suspect every purple passage is intentional. In my experience purple things are a conspicuous straining upward of the mind." (Richards, p. 186). *Seven Pillars* becomes "to my mind, redhot with passion, throughout" (*L*, 542) according to Lawrence, but this is not quite true. The fact is, that although his personality is reflected in every style in the book to a greater or lesser degree, it is his romantic Arab veil that is "redhot with passion, throughout" while his cooler, more analytical British veil is sometimes overrational and calm. By arranging his styles across a spectrum of the amount of personality they contain, we see the full range of Lawrence's psyche and ability as a writer.

IV   *Styles*

When we speak of the "amount of personality" in each of Lawrence's styles, what we mean is the *degree of involvement* of Lawrence in his subject matter that the reader detects by observing stylistic features. If the prose is highly complex, involuted and "gummy" (to use Forster's term), Lawrence is too deeply involved in his subject matter to view it objectively—and this is the case with his chapters on his own personality, 99, 100, and 103. If the prose is full of closely observed details but is basically clear and cool, we have the strange mixture of involvement and detachment that we get in scenes of horrors, like the beating at Deraa and the Turkish military barracks, and the earlier execution of Hamed.

If, on the other hand, the prose is cool, lacking in highly colored adjectives, and composed of simple elements rather than many interlocking parallel elements, then we have the analytical distance of the Lawrence who considers military alternatives or views the Arab Revolt only as a tool for British victory or describes the desert: but even in these instances of relative uninvolvement we should notice that some amount of involvement, of personality, is always present, that Lawrence never wrote one sentence that did not indicate some kind of involvement, at least in *Seven Pillars*. We can call those styles in which a relatively high degree of involvement is indicated Lawrence's "Arab veil" styles; and those which reveal distance and detachment, his "British veil" styles. Arranged in a spectrum, the styles look like this:

Maximum
involvement
and introspection

*Lawrence's Arab Veil*₃

1. Reflective: Chapters 99, 100, 103—Lawrence's personality.
2. Romantic: "Strangeness and Pain," Death of Ferraj, "S. A." poem, Charge of Tallal, Portraits of Feisal and Auda
3. Horrorific: Torture at Deraa, Massacre at Tafas, Turkish barracks at Damascus, Execution of Hamed
4. Action Narrative: Blowing up railway, Rush on Akaba, Battle of Tafileh

Lawrence's British Veil

5. Patriotic: British desire to better world (Introductory chapter); Allenby; Capture of Jerusalem
6. Descriptive: desert, seasons
7. Strategic: Chapter 33, "House of War"
8. Historical-Analytical: Syria in Chapters 4 and 58; Criticism of Feisal, Arab Revolt, and British commanders before Allenby

Minimum
involvement
and introspection

By examining closely small samples of Lawrence's styles, beginning with the total involvement of style (1) and ending with the relative coolness and detachment of style (8), we will see exactly how Lawrence projects his personality in *Seven Pillars of Wisdom*.

Style 1: (Reflective)

True there lurked always that Will uneasily waiting to burst out. My brain was sudden and silent as a wild cat, my senses like mud clogging its feet, and my self (conscious always of itself and its shyness) telling the beast it was bad form to spring and vulgar to feed on the kill. So meshed in nerves and hesitation, it could not be a thing to be afraid of; yet it was a real beast, and this book its mangy skin, dried, stuffed and set up squarely for men to stare at. (S, 564).

This "gummy" style indicates that Lawrence cannot describe himself because he does not understand himself fully; he is too close to his own personality to see it objectively. From this passage, one understands that Lawrence fears his tendency toward domination, but feels that it is healthily impeded by some inherent timidity or lack of nerve. But it is hard to grasp his division of his personality, and the striking simile of the wild cat does not help much. How is his "brain" a different sphere than his "senses" and his "self?" And how, exactly, do his "senses like mud" slow down his brain and/or his will to domination? Is *Seven Pillars* the "mangy skin" of the cat of his brain or his will, or both? We cannot see the cat through the bag of his confused and confusing style. Lawrence's use of violent metaphor and simile—always in evidence in the "Arab veil" styles—has run away with itself, and the paragraph remains lively and tensed if not fully understandable. In this veil, Lawrence seeks always to excite and unseat the reader, to force his mind to make unfamiliar connections. Sometimes it does not work; but the reader always receives a definite sense of Lawrence's own dislocation.

Style 2: (Romantic)

The everlasting battle stripped from us care of our own lives or of others'. We had ropes about our necks, and on our heads prices which showed that the enemy intended hideous tortures for us if we were caught. Each day some of us passed; and the living knew themselves just sentient puppets on God's stage: indeed, our taskmaster was merciless, merciless, so long as our bruised feet could stagger forward on the road. The weak envied those tired enough to die; for success looked so remote, and failure a near and certain, if sharp, release from toil. We lived always in the stretch or sag of nerves, either on the crest or in the trough of waves of feeling. This impotency was bitter to us, and made us live only for the seen horizon, reckless what spite we inflicted or endured, since physical sensation showed itself meanly transient. Gusts of cruelty, perversions, lusts ran lightly over the surface without troubling us; for the moral laws which had seemed to hedge about these silly accidents must be yet fainter words. We had learned that there were pangs too sharp, griefs too deep, ecstasies too high for our finitive selves to register. When emotion reached this pitch the mind choked; and memory went white till the circumstances were humdrum once more. (*S*, 29–30)

Here we see Lawrence's full romantic identification with the strangeness, pain, and adventure of the Arab Revolt. A microcosm of the structure of the book as a whole, this paragraph keeps the reader moving from peak to trough to peak of waves of emotion. Ellipsis, parallelism, colored adjectives, and adverbs, extreme images and a

strangely passive attitude on the part of the human actors make this
passage "redhot with passion, throughout." Ellipsis, or a condensation of sentence structure by omission of conjunctions and pronouns,
operates everywhere to give a breathless effect of overpowering
movement: "We had ropes about our necks, and on our heads [there
were] prices . . ."; "and the living knew themselves [to be] just
sentient puppets"; "Gusts of cruelty, perversions, [and] lusts. . . ."
Parallel, balanced elements ("our taskmaster . . . our bruised feet";
"merciless, merciless") of every sentence are piled on one another to
illustrate the accumulation of perceptions which floods the mind.
Extreme adjectives and adverbs ("everlasting battle," "hideous tortures," "bruised feet," "pangs too sharp, griefs too deep, ecstasies too
high") enforce the effect of heights and depths of waves of feeling. The
images are similarly extreme: men with ropes round their necks, a
"merciless, merciless" taskmaster, the stretch and sag of nerves,
gusts of cruelty, perversions, lusts. The rhythm within each sentence
is carefully controlled to create the essential pattern of waves and
troughs: "We lived always in the strétch or ság *of nerves,* either on the
crést or in the tróugh *of waves of feeling.*" If we count the number of
heavy caesuras in the sentences of this paragraph of nine sentences,
we find the following pattern: 0–1–5–4–1–3–4–3–1. Thus, the first
two, the fifth, and the last sentences of the paragraph represent rest
stops, troughs, in the building, forward movement, and final breaking of the wave of the paragraph, when the mind "chokes" and
memory goes "white" on the material provided by the senses.
Through it all, the men are acted upon rather than active themselves:
the battle strips from them care of their lives; the taskmaster (God?)
forces them on; impotency makes them live only for the seen horizon.
The accumulation of perceptions and powerful feelings runs out of
their control, beyond their ability to register. All grows out of the evil
"inherent in our circumstances" (S, 29), and enforces the writer's idea
that the forces of circumstance and environment were too powerful to
act against, that the men are blown "like dead leaves in the wind"
(S, 29). Totally identified with the adventure, unable to resist the pull of
the Arab veil, which involves romantic death and heroism as well as
homosexual love and masochism, Lawrence "gives himself" to "be a
possession of aliens" (S, 31) at the end of this chapter. Even as he
warns us against doing what he has done, Lawrence's attraction to and
involement in the Arab veil show clearly in his romantic style.

Lawrence's romantic style has earned him more blame than praise.
No doubt, it is "purple" and "overwritten" by contemporary stan-

dards, perhaps by any standards, but *beautifully so*. Very few writers could achieve Lawrence's powerful romantic effects, and if he sometimes overshoots the mark, well so does F. Scott Fitzgerald. We would agree I think that the passage of *The Great Gatsby*, another neo-romantic product of the 1920s, in which Nick steps into Daisy's house to find that "A breeze blew through the room, blew curtains in at one end and out the other like pale flags, twisting them up toward the frosted wedding-cake of the ceiling, and then rippled over the wine-coloured rug, making a shadow on it as wind does the sea" (Harmondsworth, 1972, p. 14) is also rather top heavy with colored adjectives. But I think we would also agree that we would not want it changed under any circumstances. And the same goes for Lawrence's romantic style. In my experience, few students and casual readers—as opposed to critics—have not been charmed by it. In the end, we have a matter of personal taste, rather than objective critical judgment, on this point.

Style 3: (Horrorific)

To keep my mind in control I numbered the blows, but after twenty lost count, and could feel only the shapeless weight of pain, not tearing claws, for which I had prepared, but a gradual cracking apart of my whole being by some too-great force whose waves rolled up my spine till they were pent within my brain, to clash horribly together. Somewhere in the place a cheap clock ticked loudly, and it distressed me that their beating was not in its time. I writhed and twisted, but was held so tightly that my struggles were useless. After the corporal ceased, the men took up, very deliberately, giving me so many, and then an interval, during which they would squabble for the next turn, ease themselves, and play unspeakably with me. This was repeated often, for what may have been no more than ten minutes. Always for the first of every new series, my head would be pulled round, to see how a hard white ridge, like a railway, darkening slowly into crimson, leaped over my skin at the instant of each stroke, with a bead of blood where the two ridges crossed. (*S,* 444)

Lawrence pays for destroying the Turkish railway with punishment that reminds him of that railway written across his back. In the closely observed, clinical detail the reader senses Lawrence's involvement as well as detachment from this event. He has both a tropistic, masochistic interest in the precise details of his pain and degradation which he views as if it were happening to someone else, and also a very real and painful awareness of the destruction of his integrity, his wholeness, by this beating and disgust and repulsion from it.

Style 4: (Action Narrative)

Out of the darkness came shattering crashes and long, loud metallic clangings of ripped steel, with many lumps of iron and plate; while one entire wheel of a locomotive whirled up suddenly black out of the cloud against the sky, and sailed musically over our heads to fall slowly and heavily into the desert behind. (S, 367)

In this passage of very clear and sensuous writing, the contrast between the soft *o* sounds and the sharp *r*, *t*, *l*, and *c* sounds provides a textbook example of Tennysonian orchestration of alliteration and assonance. We hear the sounds and watch the wheel falling, as if in a film. Only Lawrence's sensitive and artistic temperament could have caught this objective and powerful action so delicately and reported it in such an interesting, semicomical way. We feel the involvement of Lawrence's finely tuned senses and eye for the incongruous behind every phrase.

Style 5: (Patriotic)

While I was with him, word came from Chetwode that Jerusalem had fallen; and Allenby made ready to enter in the official manner which the catholic imagination of Mark Sykes had devised. He was good enough, although I had done nothing for the success, to let Clayton take me along as his staff officer for the day. The personal Staff tricked me out in their spare clothes till I looked like a major in the British Army. Dalmeny lent me red tabs, Evans his brass hat; so that I had the gauds of my appointment in the ceremony of the Jaffa gate, which for me was the supreme moment of the war. (S, 453)

This is the supreme moment of the *British* war for Lawrence; he is happy to be at Allenby's side in conquered Jerusalem, but his matter-of-fact prose reveals that the formal British side of his personality is mundane and holds no special excitement for him. It is a very quiet "supreme moment" compared to the "supreme embrace" of Arab youths "quivering together in the yielding sand" (S, 30).

Style 6: (Descriptive)

The trees and bushes stood somewhat apart, in clusters, their lower branches cropped by hungry camels. So they looked cared for, and had a premeditated air, which felt strange in the wilderness, more especially as the Tehama hitherto had been a sober bareness. (S, 79)

On one hand, this is good, clear, "objective" description which captures the look of lone trees in the Tehama region. On the other, only a sensitive temperament would have been able to feel and put into words the "strange" and "premeditated air" of the trees. The passage becomes subjective and disquieting to a certain degree, while remaining objective.

Style 7: (Strategic)

In military theory I was tolerably read, my Oxford curiosity having taken me past Napoleon to Clauswitz and his school, to Caemmerer and Moltke, and the recent Frenchmen. They had all seemed to be one-sided; and after looking at Jomini and Willisen, I had found broader principles in Saxe and Guibert and the eighteenth century. (*S,* 188)

A textbook treatise on guerrilla warfare includes this almost biblical list which impresses the reader with the quantity of names dropped, and Lawrence's "tolerably read" enforces an impression of show-offiness. Lawrence's account of a rather dry subject is not at all dry because of the amount of sheer personality in it; Lawrence even turns his theory of warfare into a religious event: "Ours seemed unlike the ritual of which Foch was priest . . ." (*S,* 190).

Style 8: (Historical-Analytical)

From childhood they were lawless, obeying their fathers only from physical fear; and their government later for much the same reason: yet few races had the respect of the upland Syrian for customary law. All of them wanted something new, for with their superficiality and lawlessness went a passion for politics, a science fatally easy for the Syrian to smatter, but too difficult for him to master. They were discontented always with what government they had; such being their intellectual pride; but few of them honestly thought out a working alternative, and fewer still agreed on one. (*S,* 335)

Lawrence writes a cool, distinguished prose here, smooth but strangely muted when one considers Lawrence's love of Syria, which makes him "sick" to think of Damascus burning at the end of the revolt. He cannot work himself into any enthusiasm, or play on all the keys of style that he reserves for the Arab veil. The comparative dryness of this paragraph indicates Lawrence's lack of identification with the subject and that his cold, clear British veil is firmly in place.

V *Summing Up*

Lawrence's stylistic spectrum reveals much of the man as he saw himself during the period of the Arab Revolt. But as much as he manages to project through the formal elements of *Seven Pillars,* a good part of his personality remains veiled, hidden, and impervious to scholarly unraveling—just as he intended it to be. Each reader must create his own Lawrence, perhaps after his own image, and this effect may be Lawrence's greatest achievement as an artist. Whichever Lawrence the reader takes away from *Seven Pillars of Wisdom* will be one of the greatest characters in all literature.

CHAPTER 7

The Mint: *Autobiography as Film*

I *Content*

LIKE Lawrence's life after Arabia, when he joined the R.A.F. as a private, then the Tank Corps and then the R.A.F again, *The Mint* is an artistic and spiritual anticlimax. The story of recruit training and the new air force (Lawrence eliminated any reference to his Tank Corps experience in the interest of artistic unity) cannot equal in excitement of exotic appeal the fantastic tale of the Arab Revolt and the "two veils" contained in *Seven Pillars of Wisdom*. In *The Mint*, we have only the British veil—in plot line at any rate—and a more constricted one than in *Seven Pillars*. Instead of grand strategy, interesting description of exotic scenery and equally exotic historical events and the pressures of war, *The Mint* contains only the daily hardship of basic training and Lawrence's feeling of the importance of air travel. Neither the men nor the events—internal and external—match the keyed-up excitement of the earlier book, and the deliberately antiromantic style of clipped sentences and abrupt chapters reveals the new straitjacketed constriction of the life of the narrator-protagonist. By joining the R.A.F., Lawrence deliberately forced himself into a "mint" which would amputate his will and hold his fragmented self together with external pressure. Unfortunately, as a literary character he is much more interesting when the pressure of strangeness, pain, and war causes his personality to come apart at the seams, and when his struggle to hold himself together is embodied in a wide variety of styles and situations. *The Mint* follows "a hard act to follow," *Seven Pillars,* and by contrast is simply too attenuated and narrow a view of life—despite the adventure of speed and air—to excite strong partisanship.

At the same time that we make this comparative artistic judgment, we should bear in mind that *The Mint* contains the important story of Lawrence's reintegration as a person and his reintegration into society—somewhat analogous to Henry Fleming's journey into himself in Crane's *Red Badge of Courage* and Ishmael's reconciliation with man and nature in *Moby Dick*[1]—of his reconciliation with his own body and psyche and that of other human beings through a newfound opening of the sense of touch, hitherto experienced only with Dahoum if at all. *The Mint* thus completes the process of alienation and detachment with a joyous fulfillment unglimpsed in *Seven Pillars*.

Like *Seven Pillars, The Mint* is clearly a poetic autobiography, in which we glimpse aspects of the narrator-protagonist's personality even more clearly than in the earlier book; ultimately however he remains a mystery. The central question of *why* he joined the R.A.F. as a private is imperfectly answered, and the book thus contains an element almost as shadowy as the S. A. and Deraa stories of *Seven Pillars*. Again like *Seven Pillars, The Mint* contains first and foremost the story of Lawrence's personality rather than that of recruit training or the development of the air force. All events in the book are seen through his eyes, filtered through his personality, and the spotlight shines fully only on him. This is not the tale of any man undergoing training, but that of T. E. Lawrence, or Ross, or Shaw, the fallen colonel, submitting himself to a new but inherently less interesting and exciting trial of self-control and willful self-debasement.

As in *Seven Pillars*, the core of *The Mint* is a personal chapter (*M*, pt. 2 chap. 19), "Odd Man Out," in which Lawrence analyzes the elements of his character in clearer language than he does in the "Myself" chapter of *Seven Pillars*. We notice the same elements; a love of physical testing and the power to withstand pain; the intellectual shyness and selfconsciousness that makes life in public a torture *and* the forcing of the self into public life, again as a test; fear of failing to measure up to impossible, absolute physical and mental standards that only Lawrence could set for himself; a fear of sexuality and touch which is largely resolved by the end of Part 3; and a fascination with pain and degradation, shown especially in the portrait of "Our Commanding Officer" (*M*, pt. 1, chap. 20); and finally an aestheticism which informs his whole view of his surroundings.

The difference in personal content between the two books is that *The Mint* presents an experiment, Lawrence's conscious attempt to "end his civil war and live the open life, patent for everyone to read" (*M*, 27). He wants to overcome his fears and fragmentation and amazingly succeeds by the end of the book. At first, Lawrence is worried about his ability to "plunge crudely amongst crude men" (*M*, 27) and to become their comrade and partner. By the end of the second section of the book, he cannot call his experiment a success even though he has been "In the Mill" with these men for a long time; his isolated, introverted nature persists: "For I have learned solidarity with them here. Not that we are very like, or will be. I joined in high hope of sharing their tastes and manners and life: but my nature persists in seeing all things in the mirror of itself, and not with a direct eye" (*M*, 195). He is still cut off from his own body as well: "Touch? I do not know. I fear and shun touch most, of my senses" (*M*, 127). In his typically puritanical tone, which equates sexuality—both masculine and heterosexual—with beastliness, Lawrence states that he has not had voluntary sexual experience (*M*, 128). Thus his relationship with Dahoum may have been only idealized, rather than overt, and his journey into touch very limited.

Until the last section of *The Mint*, Lawrence remains apart from nature. In *Seven Pillars*, nature was portrayed as a beautiful but essentially foreign and treacherous force which posed a continual threat to man:

> The crags were capped in nests of domes, less hotly red than the body of the hill; rather grey and shallow. They gave the finishing semblance of Byzantine architecture to this irresistible place: this processional way greater than imagination. The Arab armies would have been lost in the length and breadth of it, and within the walls a squadron of aeroplanes could have wheeled in formation. Our little caravan grew self-conscious, and fell dead quiet, afraid and ashamed to flaunt its smallness in the presence of the stupendous hills.[2]

Even technology, the airplane, cannot place nature in a balance with man, and the comparison with Byzantine architecture (besides being very appropriate, for there are many ruined Byzantine cities in the desert, as *The Wilderness of Zin* demonstrates) actually emphasizes man's smallness. Lawrence, uncompromising in his search for the absolute in *Seven Pillars*, finds something humiliating and degrading in nature's ability to dwarf man. In *The Mint*, however, the R.A.F. allows Lawrence to feel that the airplane *can* forge a balance between nature and man; he uses technology for an attainable goal: "The darling partiality of Nature, which has reserved across the ages her last element for us to dompt! By our handling of this, the one big new thing, will our time be judged" (*M*, 218). Still, until the very end of *The Mint*, he clearly prefers technology to nature: "A skittish motor-

bike with a touch of blood in it is better than all the riding animals on
earth, because of its logical extension of our faculties, and the hint,
the provocation to excess conferred by is honeyed untiring smooth-
ness" (M, 245).

In addition to the old divisions between man and nature, man and
other men, and Lawrence and his body that persist until the very end
of *The Mint*, we have Lawrence's most agonizing division as well: that
between parts of his own mind:

> I watch, detachedly . . . judging myself now carried away by instinct, now
> ruling a course by reason, now deciding intuitively: always restlessly
> cataloguing each aspect of my unity. . . .
> There it goes again: the conflict of mind and spirit. . . . Man, who was born
> as one, breaks into little prisms when he thinks: but if he passes through
> thought into despair, or comprehension, he again achieves some momentary
> onenesses with himself. And not only that. He can achieve a oneness of
> himself with his fellows: and of them with the stocks and stones of his
> universe: and of all the universes with the illusory everything (if he be
> positive) or with the illusory nothing (if he be nihilist) according as the
> digestive complexion of his soul be dark or fair. (M, 178–79)

As in *Seven Pillars,* Lawrence characteristically splits his mind into
several parts. But there is something new here: his glimpse of the
possibility of an almost mystical unity beyond all the parts. For the
first time, Lawrence realizes that he has the chance to feel at one with
nature, fellows, and himself.

This new opportunity is miraculously achieved in the last pages of
The Mint. As a result of his R.A.F., experience, Lawrence can
portray himself for the first and only time in his spiritual journey as a
completely fulfilled and happy human being:

> We were too utterly content to speak, drugged with an absorption fathoms
> deeper than physical contentment. Just we lay there spread-eagled in a mesh
> of bodies, pillowed on one another and sighing in happy excess of relaxation.
> The sunlight poured from the sky and melted into our tissues. From the turf
> below our moist backs there came up a sister-heat which joined us to it. Our
> bones dissolved to become a part of this underlying indulgent earth, whose
> mysterious pulse throbbed in every tremor of our bodies. The scents of the
> thousand-acre drome mixed with the familiar oil-breath of our hangar, nature
> with art. . . . (M, 249)

Lawrence has learned to reach out, touch, and lose himself in nature
and other men, to free himself from the self-consciousness which
plagued him up to this point.

The final passage of *The Mint* is a lyrical triumph in which Lawrence manages to work his austere self-deprivation and mystical sense of oneness with nature into a perfect synthesis:

And airmen are cared for as little as they care. Their simple eyes, out-turned; their natural living; the penurious imaginations which neither harrow nor reap their lowlands of mind: all these expose them, like fallows, to the processes of air. In the summer we are easily the sun's. In winter we struggle undefended along the roadway, and the rain and wind chivy us, till soon we are wind and rain. We race over in the first dawn to the College's translucent swimming pool, and dive into the elastic water which fits our bodies closely as a skin:—and we belong to that too. Everywhere a relationship: no loneliness any more. (*M*, 249–50)

This is the true conclusion of the long and hard spiritual journey which actually begins with the first page of *Seven Pillars* and continues to the last page of *The Mint*.

Lawrence's success and happiness in Cadet College (Part 3) have been questioned by critics and skeptical friends. For instance, Forster describes the change from the unhappiness and misery of Parts 1 and 2 to the contentment of Part 3 as a "transition into another medium, into a sort of comforting bath water, where I sat contented and surprised, but not convinced that I was being cleansed" (*Letters to T. E.*, p. 67). But he admits that

The two most brilliant terms are—after all—in Part III: Queen Alexandria, [sic] and the chapter that follows her—"Dance-Night"—which is so charming, so pretty: these are actually the words I must use. All through the book there's charm: lovely the descriptions of the Park, the Hangar, the final wait in the grass, and much of the smut. (*Letters to T. E.*, p. 68)

And V. S. Pritchett prefers "the remaining forty pages, based on letters" of Part 3, which "are both happier in themselves and more freely written," and contain "an excellent description of speeding on a motorbike" (Pritchett, p. 290). *Seven Pillars* has made Lawrence's distress so intimate and interesting to us that we are reluctant to accept the fact that he actually reconciled his fragments, solved his civil war, and became on the whole happy; but his letters make plain that such was the case, that he was very reluctant to leave the R.A.F. and that at some intellectual expense became to a large degree the gifted but normal R.A.F. mechanic who wrote "A Handbook to the 37½ Foot Motor Boats of the 200 Class" (1933). In 1934, he writes

John Buchan that he is resigning from the R.A.F. because of his age, "But if I could have remained perpetually young, nothing would have pleased me better" than to remain enlisted. And in a fragment from a projected sequel to *The Mint* he states this even more clearly: "The wrench this is; I shall feel like a lost dog when I leave—or when it leaves me, rather, for the R.A.F. goes on. The strange attraction in the feel of the clothes, the work, the companionship. A direct touch with men, obtained in no other way in life." (*L*, 854).

Lawrence's sincerity in making these statements and in writing the conclusion to *The Mint* may be called into question by critics who have not themselves been in the army, and who are therefore skeptical about the positive aspects of army experience about which Lawrence writes so simply and truly. Military service can in fact offer the kind of comradeship and satisfaction that would be available in no other way to an intellectual like Lawrence. The fact that two excellent critics have found the most sincere and direct writing in the book in its third section further substantiates the feeling of Lawrence's honesty that the reader experiences in this section. Fortunately or unfortunately, intelligent readers frequently prefer their heroes to remain unhappy rather than totally fulfilled at the end of a book. Ironically, the personal happiness revealed in *The Mint* makes far less interesting reading than the intense and exotic suffering that forms the basis of *Seven Pillars*. Perhaps it is true that suffering is essential to the highest art.

II   *Technique and Form*

In addition to the difference in content, *The Mint* displays two formal differences from *Seven Pillars:* the use of the present tense and the tight, clipped style including the brief, abrupt chapters. *Seven Pillars* was composed under the pressure of immediate recollection, but apart from dialogue, it is written in the past tense. Since *The Mint* is transcribed directly from notes written on the spot (in its first two sections) and from notes and letters at a somewhat greater distance in time (in its third section), Lawrence chooses present-tense narration throughout. For instance, he writes "Every man in the hut, bar me, tries shamelessly or shamefully to sing and hum and whistle" (*M*, 47), or "We grumble at the food . . ." (*M*, 160), or "Tim is the Flight Commander. He's a jewel" (*M*, 215). Thus *The Mint* is autobiography that tends in the direction of the diary, and it gains a certain immediacy as a result. Its strikingly etched, memorable scenes are not mirror images of reality, but rather photographs taken through the distorting lens of his personality, and they have the immediate impact of photographs. At the same time, the narrator-protagonist takes a retrospective view of the process he has undergone when he writes "For I have learned solidarity with them here. Not that we are very like, or will be. I joined in high hope of sharing their tastes and manners and life: but my nature persists in seeing all things in the mirror of itself, and not with a direct eye" (*M*, 195). Here, at the end of Part 2, the narrator's consciousness has shaped all the preceding immediate photographs into a pattern. This "ideological shape," lacking in *Seven Pillars* except as the reader supplied it, actually makes *The Mint* a less interesting book: the more Lawrence's character and process of change are defined, the less reader participation that is necessary.

The effect of the stringing together of this series of distorted photos and the summing up of their meaning, as Lawrence does in the quotation above, is like that of a documentary film narrated from a certain point of view, with a certain message to impress, very immediate but restricted in content—like an unusually artistic military training film in fact. This filmlike immediacy is also the result of the book's style of writing. Clipped, abrupt, generally lacking in but not without rich diction, Lawrence's style in *The Mint* keeps us rivetted to the surface of immediate events rather than propelled to airy heights of thought or writhing in involuted uneasiness. Lawrence chose this style deliberately to express the new constriction of his self, and his changed circumstances:

I'd put the *Mint* a little higher than that: and say that its style well fitted its subject: our dull clothed selves; our humdrum, slightly oppressed lives; our tight uniforms: the constriction, the limits, the artificial conduct, of our bodies and minds and spirits, in the great machine which the R.A.F. is becoming. I had to hold myself down, on each page, with both hands.

A painted or sentimental style, such as I used in *The Seven Pillars*, would have been out of place in the *Mint*, except in the landscape passages, where I have used it. (*L*, 596)

Within the basic attenuation, there is a certain amount of stylistic variation in *The Mint*. Though clearer than similar passages in *Seven Pillars*, "gummy" reflective passages sometimes appear:

Man, who was born as one, breaks into little prisms when he thinks: but if he passes through thought into despair, or comprehension, he again achieves

some momentary onenesses with himself. And not only that. He can achieve
a oneness of himself with his fellows: and of them with the stocks and stones
of his universe: and of all the universes with the illusory everything (if he be
positive) or with the illusory nothing (if he be nihilist) according as the
digestive complexion of his soul be dark or fair. (*M*, 179)

His aesthetic temperament continually shapes his surroundings in its
own expressionistic image: "So the beams and ties of the roof-trusses
are tonight futurist and mysterious, being pendent with all our
equipment, slung up there to dry stiff, after scrubbing" (*M*, 48). He is
as good at describing action as ever, and the first short sentences help:

A glance at the speedometer: seventy-eight. Boanerges is warming up. I pull
the throttle right open, on the top of the slope, and we swoop flying across the
dip, and up-down up-down the switchback beyond: the weighty machine
launching itself like a projectile with a whirr of wheels into the air at the
take-off of each rise, to land lurchingly with such a snatch of the driving chain
as jerks my spine like a rictus. (*M*, 242)

And his dialogue is very fine, and rings true: " 'Do you know what
happened to me, tonight? I met a girl . . . or she wasn't a girl, really
. . . and we . . . clicked and went off together. Remember that dollar
I borrowed off you, Monday? Well that just did it' " (*M*, 223–24). But
the powerful, colored, high romantic touch is gone, and we miss it
very much, as we do the whole Arab veil of adventure and strangeness.

Obviously, this book of "notes" has taken much work to polish—as
the British Library manuscripts of *The Mint* prove—and is an artistic
autobiography, in which we feel what it was like to be T. E.
Lawrence–Ross–Shaw in his new situation. The fact that this new
situation is not nearly as interesting as the old, and that Lawrence's
personality is less pressured and consequently less divided and
mysterious for us, should not blind us to an interesting experiment in
autobiographical form. For *The Mint* is poetic autobiography, but in
the form of a documentary film, complete with distorting lenses, a
series of sharp frames (or chapters) moving past us, rather than a rich
deep mysterious self-portrait in oils. As Lawrence pointed out in a
letter to Mrs. Shaw in the British Library collection, neither *The Mint*
nor *Seven Pillars* owes anything to Joyce. But in its fast-moving
immediacy, as in its paean to the air force, *The Mint* remains a tribute
to twentieth-century technology. It is the first autobiography to meet
the film on its own ground.

CHAPTER 8

Further Arabians

THANKS to the diligent work of Jeffrey Meyers and the Weintraubs, the extent of Lawrence's influence *as a character* on the literature of the twentieth century has been clearly established. Numerous writers have based whole poems and novels on the Lawrence character. More writers have mentioned him tangentially in their work. This is actually a measure of Lawrence's literary ability, for most of these poems and novels have been influenced by the character Lawrence that he created himself in *Seven Pillars* and *The Mint*, rather than by T. E. Lawrence the man, himself.

As one of the most fascinating self-created characters ever conceived, fully on a par with Henry Adams' Henry Adams, Norman Mailer's Norman Mailer of *The Armies of the Night*, and the Thoreau of *Walden*, Lawrence or a reasonable facsimile thereof has appeared in poems by Altounyan, Auden, Graves, MacLeish, and Rodman. In drama, he has been the model for Ransom in Auden and Isherwood's *The Ascent of F.6*, for Shaw's Private Meek and Saint Joan, and for Rattigan's Ross. He provided the impetus for Rudolf Valentino's Sheik, and served more recently as the subject of Robert Bolt's film *Lawrence of Arabia*. Novelists have made even more use of Lawrence than have the poets, dramatists, and filmmakers. He has featured in thin disguise in James Aldridge's *Heroes of the Empty View*, Maurice Barrès' *Un Jardin sur l'oronte*, John Buchan's *Courts of the Morning*, André Malraux's *The Walnut Trees of Altenburg*, and as late as 1970, in Anthony West's *David Rees Among Others*. C. Day Lewis made use of Lawrence's figure for a detective story, *Shell of Death*, and even D. H. Lawrence, the namesake who never reciprocated T. E.'s openly expressed admiration of him, makes some deprecatory remarks about a "Colonel C. E. Florence" in *Lady Chatterley's Lover*.

While such evidence provides a tribute to Lawrence's creation of an interesting character—himself—it tells us very little about the

145

direct artistic influence that Lawrence has had on later writers. Although these writers of poems, dramas, films, and novels obviously owe the inspiration for the characters in some of their work to Lawrence, we can scarcely say that he influenced the style, structure, or form of any of their creations, including those in which he appears. Has his artistic influence then been confined to myth and nebulous inspiration, a father without any heirs in the direct line of descent, or has he in fact pointed the way for other literary artists to write their own work?

If we look to the writers in the tradition in which Lawrence himself wrote, we get a very clear answer to that question. All three of the greatest Anglo-Arabian travelers and travelwriters after Lawrence are directly indebted to him for important bits of the content of their works; and at least one of them has been obviously and deeply influenced by his artistry. The fact that Bertram Thomas, Harry St. John Bridger Philby, and Wilfred Thesiger all held Lawrence in the highest respect as an authority on the desert and desert ways certainly argues conclusively for the truth of his account of the Arabs. After Doughty and Lawrence, the last great unknown in Arabian travel was the difficult Rub al Khali, or Empty Quarter, which no European had ever crossed, so treacherous were its hardships for the traveler. In February, 1931, Bertram Thomas became the first to accomplish this great feat, and was closely followed by Philby, who took an even more difficult route, in the same year. In 1946–1947 and 1947–1948, Wilfred Thesiger crossed the Empty Quarter twice, covering areas not explored by his predecessors.

Lawrence's introduction, generous in the praise of the traveler (for whom Lawrence tried to secure a knighthood [L, 714]), graces Thomas' Arabia Felix. In his preface to his work, Thomas cites Lawrence as a "friend," to whom he turned for editorial reading. Philby scatters respectful references to Lawrence throughout his many books on Arabia, citing him more than twenty times in his Arabian Days (1948) alone. And Thesiger, in his brilliant Arabian Sands (Harmondsworth, 1959), openly quotes Lawrence directly on several occasions as an authority on matters of Arab customs.

Although Lawrence respected both Thomas—who disproved Lawrence's own idea of surveying the Empty Quarter by airship—and Philby as travelers, he thought them inferior writers when compared to other "Arabians" like Palgrave for instance, as we saw in the second chapter of this study. In a letter written in 1933, Lawrence classes Philby and Thomas as great explorers, but calls Palgrave a

great explorer *and* writer (*L*, 768). And in his foreward to Thomas'
book, he carefully refrains from praising Thomas' literary art, except
for a suspect single sentence: "Thomas let me read the draft, and I
then did my best to comment usefully; once remarking that the tale
was good enough for his journey—no faint judgement, set against
which I think the finest thing in Arabian exploration." This praise is
faint indeed if we remember the extravagent praise that Lawrence
lavishes on the artist Doughty in his foreward to *Arabia Deserta.*
Thomas completed his journey in February, 1931; he completed his
book by December, 1931, according to its preface. Philby wrote
with journalistic ease and rapidity. If we recall that Doughty spent
ten years working his notes into literature, that Lawrence's book was
the result of seven years of writing and revision, and that Thesiger's
Arabian Sands appeared nine years after his travels, we have a clue to
Lawrence's relatively negative assessment of the artistic merit of the
Philby and Thomas books.

Ironically, Lawrence thought Thomas the last great Arabian
traveler because he had explored the last barrier the country afforded, but Wilfred Thesiger, much closer than Thomas to Lawrence
in style and spirit, proved him wrong by covering new territory.
Although Lawrence influenced Thomas and Philby in indirect ways,
Thesiger remains Lawrence's true and direct artistic heir. This
influence on the form and content of Thesiger's book in particular
appears in several areas: (1) direct quotations used for authoritative
support; (2) intense dissatisfaction with Western civilization and a
desire to escape it; (3) a straddling of fences between Western and
Arab identities; (4) a predilection for the austerity and physical test of
the desert; (5) the use of highly colored style and dialogue; and (6) a
creative literary use of characterization. Lawrence and Thesiger are
not alone, as twentieth-century travelers, in feeling their Western
identities weakened by the attraction of Arabia: Philby actually
converted to Islam and served as King Sa'ud's adviser. And all
travelers, including Thomas, have been attracted to the physical
challenge represented by the desert. But Thesiger remains Lawrence's true and greatest heir because he alone of the three regards
the travel book as primarily an artistic form and in *Arabian Sands* has
created an enduring work of art.

In his book, Thesiger quotes or mentions Lawrence directly no less
than five times; by contrast, Doughty is not even mentioned once.
We learn that it was Lawrence's *Revolt in the Desert* that first
"awakened" Thesiger's "interest in the Arabs" (p. 39). *Arabian*

Sands' prologue includes a direct quotation from *Seven Pillars,* "Beduin ways were hard, even for those brought up in them and for strangers terrible: a death in life." Thesiger's own comment on this quotation is that "No man can live this life and emerge unchanged. He will carry, however faint, the imprint of the desert, the brand which marks the nomad; and he will have within him the yearning to return, weak or insistent according to his nature. For this cruel land can cast a spell which no temperate climate can match" (p. 15). On the Kissim Pass, Thesiger recollects and quotes approvingly Lawrence's parable about the lack of smell of the desert, and the Arabs' comments on the desert wind: " 'This,' they told him, 'is the best: it has no taste.' " In stating that "the Arabs are a race which produces its best only under conditions of extreme hardship and deteriorates progressively as living conditions become easier" (p. 97), Thesiger quotes Lawrence for substantiation. The one footnote that he places on Lawrence's book is a clarification rather than a contradiction: "Homosexuality is common among most Arabs, especially in the towns, but it is very rare among the Bedu, who of all Arabs have the most excuse for indulging in this practice, since they spend long months away from their women. Lawrence described in *Seven Pillars of Wisdom* how his escort made use of each other to slake their needs, but those men were villagers from the oasis, not Bedu" (p. 125).

In almost all these passages, as in his constant emphasis on the dangers of his journeys, Thesiger echoes Lawrence's own preoccupation with austerity and hardship. In fact, this seems to be his primary motivation for desert travels: "I went there to find peace in the hardship of the desert travel and the company of desert peoples" (p. 278). He also reveals in himself a weakened Western identity and division between England and Arabia in his affections. He like Lawrence alternates between both ways of life; on an R.A.F. base in Arabia, he says

It was a pleasant change talking English instead of the constant effort of talking Arabic; to have a hot bath and to eat well-cooked food; even to sit at ease on a chair with my legs stretched out, instead of sitting on the ground with them tucked under me. But the pleasure of doing these things was enormously enhanced for me by the knowledge that I was going back into the desert. . . . (p. 182)

Back in England, he cannot wait to be back in Arabia: "In deserts, however arid, I have never felt homesick for green fields and woods in spring, but now that I was in England I longed with an ache that was almost physical to be back in Arabia" (p. 203). Like the Lawrence caught between two cultures, Thesiger among Englishmen "knew that I stood apart from them and would never find contentment among them, whereas I could find it among these Bedu, although I should never be one of them" (p. 184). Lawrence hated the idea that the consciousness of nationalism which he helped develop in the Arabs would destroy their traditional way of life. Thesiger writes that

> Today the desert where I travelled is scarred with the tracks of lorries and littered with discarded junk imported from Europe and America. But this material desecration is unimportant compared with the demoralization which has resulted among the Bedu themselves. While I was with them they had no thought of a world other than their own. They were not ignorant savages; on the contrary, they were the lineal heirs of a very ancient civilization, who found within the framework of their society the personal freedom and self discipline for which they craved. Now they are being driven out of the desert into towns where the qualities which once gave them mastery are no longer sufficient. (pp. 11–12)

Thesiger merely chronicles the end of the process Lawrence had foreseen forty years earlier, and which is underway in Israel today as well as in all parts of the Middle East.[1]

In this, as in his total cultural relativity, Thesiger actually carries Lawrence's own thoughts and feelings to their ultimate conclusion: "I went there with a belief in my own racial superiority, but in their tents I felt like an uncouth, inarticulate barbarian, an intruder from a shoddy and materialistic world" (p. 38). Thesiger's story of his relationship with the Arabs has a happier end than that of Lawrence, who as we have seen went from extreme closeness to and appreciation of them to a bitter detachment. But Thesiger came later in time and, most important of all, did not experience the ravages of war and the deceit of politics. Lawrence was actually forced to take part in bloody killing and pillaging and "preaching" to the Beduin tribes. Thesiger steered clear of tribal politics as far as was possible, and never had to kill anyone. Compared to Lawrence he is *just* a traveler; but as such, he carries Lawrence's already relativistic cultural thought through to a worthwhile conclusion. We have traveled far in our appreciation of other cultures in our century—the full route from Doughty to Lawrence to Thesiger.

Thesiger's style also carries Lawrence's through to a more modern conclusion. He manages the great feat of retaining the same tone of

"Arabian" coloring that we noted in Lawrence's "Arab veil" writing, but writes a basically contemporary English. Desert life evokes a lyrical, delicately chivalric style of parallelism expressed in contemporary diction: "I had learnt the satisfaction which comes from hardship and the pleasure which springs from abstinence; the contentment of a full belly; the richness of meat; the taste of clean water; the ecstasy of surrender when the craving for sleep becomes a torment; the warmth of a fire in the chill of dawn" (p. 37). Subtly, he attempts to capture the syntax and rhetoric of Arabic speech in very many passages, augmenting this lean exoticism with Arabic names and words: "The Riqaishi gave his camel an angry blow and answered, 'You would not have brought the Christian here if you had wished to please me' " (p. 318). Though less pronounced than Lawrence's exoticisms, Thesiger gives us essentially an updated version of the same thing.

Perhaps most tellingly, he provides "A List of the Chief Characters on the Various Journeys" (p. 332) at the end of the book. The use of the word "characters" instead of "people" or "personalities" gives a clear hint of Thesiger's literary intentions. Although less dramatized and spectacular than Lawrence's Feisal and Auda, Thesiger's Salim bin Kabina and Salim bin Ghabaisha are in fact "chief characters" in a drama in which they emerge as vivid, fully rounded, and yet exotic central actors. The farewell between the three men, on the very last page of the book, remains as touching as any parting in Anglo-Arabian (or other) literature, and the entire story has been structured to emphasize this final passage: "The lorry arrived after breakfast. We embraced for the last time. I said, 'Go in peace,' and they answered together, 'Remain in the safe keeping of God, Umbarak.' . . . I was glad when Codrai took me to the aerodrome at Sharja. As the plane climbed over the town and swung out above the sea I knew how it felt to go into exile" (p. 330). Ostensibly restrained, each carefully chosen word of colored dialogue carries a heavy emotional weight, because we have watched the characters go through so much together and develop into human beings who come alive on the page.

Thesiger, in his own role as Umbarak and as narrator, never gives his own self completely away. As in Lawrence's case, the reader feels that there remains a lot more for the author to say about himself, if he cared to, and that despite his stated explanation for going to Arabia, the real explanation—namely, what personality trait makes him so amenable to hardship—eludes us. Thesiger thus takes his place in the grand tradition of the mysterious Anglo-Arabian travel artist.

In this comparison of Thesiger and Lawrence, we have clear evidence that Lawrence did in fact directly influence other writers *as an artist* and not merely as a character. If any spots remain for exploration in Arabia or perhaps other deserts, he may influence other writers to come. But if we truly appreciate Lawrence's work, we understand that his unique personality, position in time and his war experience make it impossible for him to have more than a very few ancestors or followers, if any. Like few men, he sat astride two centuries and barely managed to escape whole. In his person as his art, he becomes the focal point for all the vectors of East and West, colonialism and anticolonialism, war and peace, nature and technology, self and antiself, heroism and antiheroism, realism and imagination, and fiction and nonfiction of our century. He is the nodal man, who symbolizes the problem of an art form, an empire, a century, a civilization, and an attempted personal solution to this problem. This problem can be formulated as the known but pressing question of how to reconcile freedom and wholeness. Out of the swirl of clashing pressures, he fashioned a great "mystery-masterpiece" of world literature, at once typical of a tradition and totally unique. Too unusual to beget many direct artistic heirs, Lawrence holds all subsequent literary artists in his debt as the man who showed just how intriguing a character can be created in literature and who experimented boldly with autobiographical form. After half a century, it is time that both *Seven Pillars of Wisdom* and *The Mint* began to live lives of their own.

Notes and References

Chapter One

1. T. E. Lawrence, *Seven Pillars of Wisdom* (Garden City, N.Y., 1938). All references are to this edition (hereafter cited in the text as *S*), except where I specifically cite the Oxford text of 1922 and other early manuscript forms. My edition is identical with the Subscriber's Edition of 1926 except for minor details, and I frequently refer to it as the "final edition." A complete history of the many texts of *Seven Pillars* begins my fourth chapter.

2. T. E. Lawrence, *The Mint* (New York, 1955); hereafter cited in the text as *M*.

3. T. E. Lawrence, *Revolt in the Desert* (New York, 1927).

4. T. E. Lawrence, *The Letters of T. E. Lawrence*, ed. David Garnett (London, 1938), p. 513; hereafter cited in the text as *L*.

5. R. P. Blackmur, "The Everlasting Effort: A Citation of T. E. Lawrence," in *The Lion and the Honeycomb* (New York, 1955), p. 108; originally published in R. P. Blackmur, *The Expense of Greatness* (New York, 1940).

6. Richard Aldington, *Lawrence of Arabia: A Biographical Enquiry* (London, 1955), p. 330.

7. Malcolm Muggeridge, "Poor Lawrence," review of Anthony Nutting's *Lawrence of Arabia*, *New Statesman* 52 (October 27, 1961), 604

8. Stanley Weintraub, *Private Shaw and Public Shaw* (New York, 1963), p. 129.

9. Thomas J. O'Donnell, "The Dichotomy of Self in T. E. Lawrence's *Seven Pillars of Wisdom*" (Ph.D. diss., University of Illinois, 1970).

10. O'Donnell, abstract, p. 3.

11. G. Wilson Knight, "T. E. Lawrence," in *Neglected Powers* (London, 1971), pp. 309–51.

12. John S. Friedman, "The Challenge of Destiny: A Comparison of T. E. Lawrence's and André Malraux's Adventure Tales" (Ph.D. diss., New York University, 1974).

13. Quoted in Weintraub, pp. 113–14.

14. E. M. Forster, "T. E. Lawrence," in *Abinger Harvest* (London, 1936), p. 170.

15. Robert Graves, *Lawrence and the Arabs* (London, 1927), p. 407.

16. This letter appears in *Letters to T. E. Lawrence*, ed. A. W. Lawrence (London, 1962), p. 155.

17. Ibid., p. 213.

18. Ibid., p. 67.

19. L. P. Hartley, "A Failed Masterpiece," *The Listener* (April 14, 1955), 658–59.

20. V. S. Pritchett, "Ross at the Depot," in *The Living Novel & Later Appreciations* (New York, 1964), pp. 288–90.

21. See *Letters to T. E. Lawrence*, pp. 66–69 (Forster), pp. 96–98 (E. Garnett), and pp. 82–85 (D. Garnett).

22. Anonymous, "The Mint," *Kirkus* 22 (December 15, 1954), 830.

23. Michael Bograd, "T. E. Lawrence: An Appreciation of his Military Leadership" (B.A. honors paper, Ben-Gurion University of the Negev, 1974), pp. 54–5, 57.

24. In *T. E. Lawrence by his Friends*, ed. A. W. Lawrence (New York, 1963), pp. 165–67.

Chapter Two

1. William L. Howarth, "Some Principles of Autobiography," *New Literary History* (Winter, 1974), 363–81.

2. Dated October 21, 1925 in the Houghton Library series of seventy-three letters to Robert Graves.

3. *T. E. by his Friends*, p. 343.

4. *The Home Letters of T. E. Lawrence and his Brothers*, Note by M. R. Lawrence (Oxford, 1954), p. 207.

5. Charles Doughty, *Travels in Arabia Deserta*, intro. T. E. Lawrence (New York, 1936), p. 346.

6. Michael Foss, "Dangerous Guides: English Writers and the Desert," *The New Middle East*, no. 9 (June, 1969), 39.

7. Jean Beraud Villars, *T. E. Lawrence or The Search for the Absolute* (London, 1958), p. 296. This book originally appeared in French in 1955 and was translated into English by Peter Dawnay.

8. For a concise history of the Anglo-Arabian travel book, see Robin Fedden, *English Travellers in the Near East*, Writers and their Work, no. 97, ed. Bonamy Dobree (London, 1958).

9. Alexander W. Kinglake, *Eothen* (London, 1948).

10. Iran Jewett, "Kinglake and the English Travelogue of the Nineteenth Century," *Dissertation Abstracts* 25 (1964), pp. 2961–62.

11. W. H. Hudson, *Idle Days in Patagonia* (New York, 1917).

12. Letter dated November 6, 1928 in the Houghton Library collection.

13. *T. E. by his Friends*, p. 331.

14. Robert Hamilton, *W. H. Hudson: The Vision of Earth* (Port Washington, N.Y., 1970), p. 111.

15. T. E. Lawrence, Introduction to *Arabia Deserta*, pp. 17ff.

16. This review first appeared in *The Bibliophile's Almanack* (1928), pp. 35–41; reprinted in Herbert Read, *A Coat of Many Colours* (London, 1945), pp. 24–26.

17. See Hogarth, *Life of C. M. Doughty*, p. 204.

18. Doughty, II, 26.

19. Meyers, p. 84.

20. Phillip Knightley and Colin Simpson, *The Secret Lives of Lawrence of Arabia* (New York, 1970). Although this biography contains much valuable documentary evidence that is new, it merely restates in a somewhat sensationalist Lowell Thomas manner conclusions about Lawrence's life that were already known. Its one really valuable contribution may be the identification of "S. A." as Lawrence's Arab servant, Dahoum, but here as everywhere else the book is convincing rather than truly conclusive. John Mack's *A Prince of Our Disorder* (London, 1976) is a far more sober, complete and reliable work, but the mystery of Lawrence's inner workings eludes even this psychoanalyst. For Doughty, see Richard Bevis, "Spiritual Geology: C. M. Doughty and the Land of the Arabs," *Victorian Studies* 16, no. 2 (December, 1972), 163–81. Despite Bevis' brave attempt to define Doughty's ultimate motivation, the reader leaves through the same door by which he entered.

21. In "The Changing East," an article originally published anonymously by Lawrence in *The Round Table* 40 (September, 1920), 756–72; reprinted in *Oriental Assembly*, ed. A. W. Lawrence (New York, 1940), p. 73.

Chapter Three

1. See *The Letters of T. E. Lawrence*, p. 621, for the letter to Forster (August 6, 1928).

2. See Meyers, chap. 6; and the two last chapters of O'Donnell.

3. *T. E. by his Friends*, p. 240.

4. T. E. Lawrence, *T. E. Lawrence to his Biographer, Robert Graves* (New York, 1938), p. 56.

5. For the connection between the poems that Lawrence read in his *Oxford Book of English Verse* and events during the course of the revolt, see the notes in Wilson's *Minorities*. The poems Lawrence read during the revolt were Arthur O'Shaughnessy's "Ode," John Davidson's "Song," William Watson's "The Great Misgiving," Henry Cust's "Non Nobis," Kipling's "Dedication," and Clough's "Say Not the Struggle Naught Availeth."

6. *T. E. by his Friends*, p. 388.

7. The *Arab Bulletin* was a secret intelligence newsletter of Arab affairs created by Lawrence while a member of the Arab Bureau in Cairo. Lawrence's contributions to it have been reprinted under the title *Secret Despatches from Arabia*. This entry is dated February 15, 1917 (*Secret Despatches*, p. 64).

8. James A. Notopoulos, "The Tragic and the Epic in T. E. Lawrence," *Yale Review* 54 (Spring, 1965), 338.

9. Avraham Feinglass, "T. E. Lawrence and the Heroic Narrative Mode" (B.A. honors paper, Ben-Gurion University of the Negev, 1974).

10. Ibid., p.3

11. Quoted in Ibid., p. 4.

12. Ibid., p. 4.

13. See Knightley and Simpson, pp. 180–86, for a discussion of Beaumont's testimony and the whole "S. A." question.

14. He says this not only on page 128 of *The Mint*, but also in a letter of November 6, 1928 to Robert Graves (Houghton Library).

15. On a graduate paper ("A House Divided: The 'Crisis of Belief in T. E. Lawrence's *Seven Pillars of Wisdom*") that I wrote for a course he taught at the University of Connecticut in 1970, Stephen Spender commented about Lawrence that "He surely must have been at any rate a repressed homosexual. Remember his very sympathetic account of the two Arab boys who are lovers." Spender went on to comment more generally that "Lawrence was a very courageous man and experienced doubtless much of what he described, but he was not finally self-revealing and there was something about him which flirted with destiny. He is somewhere a bit false and capable of falsification." Jeffrey Meyers finds "continual evidence of homosexuality, especially with Sheik Ahmed" (Meyers, p. 123). [*Sic*—Dahoum's name was Salim Achmed, and "Sheik" is a title applied only to very honored and usually old men]. However, this "continual evidence" is oblique and circumstantial while all the evidence against overt homosexuality in Lawrence's life is direct: testimony of friends and Lawrence's own open disavowals of *all* voluntary sexual activity. I continue to believe that Lawrence was above all a puritan and only a latent homosexual who had an idealized love relationship with Dahoum, which did involve some degree of the sense of touch, but not much. For comparisons with the Queequeg-Ishmael relationship in *Moby Dick*, see my paper listed in the bibliography. In any case, this question of homosexuality while obviously important to *Seven Pillars'* interpretation in some ways and strangely fascinating to many readers, has been heavily overemphasized and detracts attention from far more significant aspects of Lawrence's life and art.

16. Quoted in J. M. Wilson's edition of *Minorities*, p. 50.

Chapter Four

1. *Abinger Harvest*, p. 165.

2. See O'Donnell, p. 31, and Meyers, chap. 3.

3. In Houghton Library, MS. Notebook fMS eng 1252 (356), Lawrence counts 217 copies; in Bertram Rota, "Lawrence of Arabia and *Seven Pillars of Wisdom*," *Texas Quarterly* 5, no. 3 (Autumn, 1962), 49, the figure of 211 copies is given. Lawrence's mysteries never cease!

4. This analogy is William Howarth's.

5. Meyers, p. 56.

6. Ibid., pp. 25–26.

7. *Secret Despatches*, p. 17. This *Arab Bulletin* report of November 18 actually describes the meeting with Feisal that took place on October 23.

8. *Secret Despatches*, p. 37.

9. Beraud Villars, p. 300.

10. Ronald Storrs, "Lawrence of Arabia," *Listener* 53 (February 3, 1955), pp. 188-89.

11. Quoted in Knightley and Simpson, p. 245.

12. Meyers, p. 61.

13. Ibid., pp. 61–62.

14. Ibid., p 62.

15. Lawrence's choice of Circassian as a surrogate identity was actually extremely clever, for the Circassians are Caucasians who speak a non-Semitic language; thus Lawrence's bad accent and poor grammar in Arabic would go unnoticed by the Turks, who themselves are not native speakers of Arabic.

16. Meyers, p. 63.

17. *Lawrence and the Arabs,* pp. 407–8.

Chapter Five

1. See Joseph Conrad, *Lord Jim* in *The Complete Works of Joseph Conrad* (Garden City, N. Y., 1924), pp. 338–39. See Lawrence's list of motives, quoted in Knightley and Simpson, pp. 178–79.

2. E. M. Forster, *A Passage to India* (New York, 1952), p. 322.

3. T. E. Lawrence, *T. E. Lawrence's Letters to H. S. Ede, 1927–35*, ed. H. S. Ede (London, 1942), p. 11.

4. Dated May 4, 1927 (British Library); quoted in O'Donnell, p. 101.

5. Dated June 10, 1927 (British Library); quoted in O'Donnell, p. 102.

6. Richard F. Burton, "Mr. Doughty's Travels," *Academy* 34 (July 28, 1888), 47–48.

7. Joseph Conrad, *Heart of Darkness,* in *Conrad's Heart of Darkness and the Critics,* ed. Bruce Harkness (Belmont, Calif., 1962), p. 36

Chapter Six

1. For further information on this interpretation, see T. E. Lawrence, *T. E. Lawrence to his Biographer, Liddell Hart* (Garden City, N. Y., 1938), p. 130.

2. In an annotation written on the inside front cover of his personal copy of Robert Vansittart's *Singing Caravan* (in the Houghton Library).

3. See Meyers, p. 85, for a description of ten styles in *Seven Pillars.* I thank Dr. Zev Bar-Lev for suggesting that Lawrence's styles could be arranged on a chart.

Chapter Seven

1. For a full comparison of Lawrence, Ishmael, and Ahab see my "T. E. Lawrence and *Moby Dick, " Research Studies* 44, no 1 (March, 1976), 1–12.

2. *Seven Pillars,* p. 351.

Chapter Eight

1. And not just in the Middle East. When Señor Emilio Rabassa, the son of the former Mexican foreign minister, visited Beersheba, he told me that he noted among the Beersheba Beduin the same cultural decay caused by encroaching Western civilization as exists among the Indians in his own country. The Indians in the United States provide yet another example of the universality of Lawrence's (and Thesiger's) depressing insights.

Selected Bibliography

PRIMARY SOURCES

1. Manuscript Collections
   Bodleian Library, Oxford.
   British Library.
   Houghton Library, Harvard University.
   University of Texas Library.

2. Books
Cancelled First Chapter of Seven Pillars of Wisdom with Sixteen Letters by Lawrence and a Memoir by Ralph Isham. New York: Viking Press, 1937.
Carchemish: Report on the Excavations at Djerabis on Behalf of the British Museum Conducted by C. Leonard Woolley, MA and T. E. Lawrence, MA. Part I. Coauthored with C. Leonard Woolley. Introduction by D. G. Hogarth. London: British Museum, 1914.
Carchemish: Report on the Excavations at Djerabis on Behalf of the British Museum Conducted by C. Leonard Woolley, MA with T. E. Lawrence, MA, and P. L. O. Guy. Part II. The Town Defenses. By C. L. Woolley with T. E. Lawrence and P. L. O. Guy. London: British Museum, 1921.
Colonel Lawrence of Arabia: His Original Manuscript Autobiography and Correspondence with Robert Graves. London: Maggs Bros., 1936.
Crusader Castles. 2 vols. London: Golden Cockerel Press, 1936.
The Diary of T. E. Lawrence MCMXI. London: Corvinus Press, 1937.
Eight Letters from T. E. Lawrence. Edited by Harley Granville-Barker, London, 1939.
An Essay on Flecker. London: Corvinus Press, 1937.
The Essential T. E. Lawrence. Edited by David Garnett. New York: Dutton, 1951.

Evolution of a Revolt: Early Post-war Writings of T. E. Lawrence. Edited by Stanley and Rodelle Weintraub. University Park, Pa.: Pennsylvania State University Press, 1968.
[J. H. Ross, translator]. *The Forest Giant* by Adrien Le Corbeau. London: Jonathan Cape, 1924.
The Home Letters of T. E. Lawrence and his Brothers. Note by M. R. Lawrence. Oxford: Basil Blackwell, 1954.
A Letter from T. E. Lawrence to his Mother. London: Corvinus Press, 1936.

Letters from T. E. Shaw to Viscount Carlow. London: Corvinus Press, 1936.

The Letters of T. E. Lawrence. Edited by David Garnett. London: Jonathan Cape, 1938.

Letters from T. E. Shaw to Bruce Rogers. New Fairfield, Conn.: Press of William Edwin Rudge, 1933.

Men in Print: Essays in Literary Criticism. Introduction by A. W. Lawrence. London: Golden Cockerel Press, 1940.

Minorities. Edited by J. M. Wilson. Preface by C. Day Lewis. London: Jonathan Cape, 1971.

The Mint. Note by A. W. Lawrence. New York: W. W. Norton, 1955.

The Mint. Preface by J. M. Wilson. Harmondsworth: Penguin, 1978.

More Letters from T. E. Shaw to Bruce Rogers. New Fairfield, Conn., 1936.

[T. E. Shaw, translator]. *The Odyssey of Homer.* London: Oxford University Press, 1955.

Oriental Assembly. Edited by A. W. Lawrence. London: Williams and Norgate, 1939.

Revolt in the Desert. New York: George Doran, 1927.

Secret Despatches from Arabia. Foreward by A. W. Lawrence. London: Golden Cockerel Press, 1939.

Selected Letters of T. E. Lawrence. Edited by David Garnett. London: Jonathan Cape, 1941.

Selections from "Seven Pillars of Wisdom." Edited John Cullen. London: James Brodie, 1940.

Seven Pillars of Wisdom: A Triumph. Garden City, N.Y.: Garden City Publishing Co., 1938.

Shaw-Ede, T. E. Lawrence's Letters to H. S. Ede 1927–1935. London: Golden Cockerel Press, 1942.

T. E. Lawrence/Fifty Letters. 1920–1935. An Exhibition. Austin: University of Texas Humanities Research Center, 1962.

T. E. Lawrence to his Biographers Robert Graves and Liddell Hart: Information about Himself in the Form of Letters, Notes, Answers to Questions and Conversations. New York: Doubleday, Doran, 1938.

[Translator]. *Two Arabic Folk Tales.* London: Corvinus Press, 1937.

The Wilderness of Zin. Coauthored with C. Leonard Woolley. London: Palestine Exploration Fund, 1915.

3. Book Reviews

[C.D. (Colin Dale)]. "A Critic of Critics Criticised." *Spectator* 139 (August 27, 1927), 321–22.

[C.D.]. "D. H. Lawrence's Novels." *Spectator* 139 (August 6, 1927), 223. Included in *Men in Print.*

[C.D.]. "Hackluyt—First Naval Propagandist." *Spectator* 139 (September 10, 1927), 390–91.

[C.D.]. "Mixed Biscuits." *Spectator* 139 (August 20, 1927), 290–91.

"The Wells Short Stories." *Spectator* 140 (February 25, 1928), 268–69. Included in *Men in Print.*

4. Literary Introductions and Prefaces
"Introduction" to *Travels in Arabia Deserta* by Charles Doughty. London:
Jonathan Cape, 1921. Pp. xxv–xxxv.
"Introduction" to *Twilight of the Gods* by Richard Garnett. London: John
Lane, 1924. Pp. vii–xiv.
"Introduction" to *Arabia Felix: Across the Empty Quarter of Arabia* by
Bertram Thomas. London: Jonathan Cape, 1932. Pp. xvii–xx.
"Preface" to Leicester Galleries, *Catalogue of an Exhibition of Paintings,
Pastels, Drawings and Woodcuts Illustrating Colonel T. E. Lawrence's
"Seven Pillars of Wisdom."* London: Leicester Galleries, 1927.
"Prefatory Letter" to *River Niger* by Simon Jesty. London: Boriswood, 1935.
Pp. 11–13.

SECONDARY SOURCES

1. Bibliographies
The journal *T. E. Lawrence Studies* should be consulted for current bibliography and research.

BAXTER, FRANK. *An Annotated Check-List of a Collection of Writings By
and About T. E. Lawrence.* Los Angeles, n.p. 1968.
CLEMENTS, FRANK, *T. E. Lawrence: a reader's guide.* Newton Abbot: David
& Charles, 1972.
DISBURY, DAVID G. *T. E. Lawrence of Arabia: A Collector's Booklist.*
Egham, Surrey, n.p. 1972.
DUVAL, ELIZABETH W. *T. E. Lawrence: A Bibliography.* New York: Arrow
Editions, 1938.
HOUSTON, GUYLA BOND. *Thomas Edward Lawrence, 1888–1935. A
checklist of Lawrenciana, 1915–65.* Stillwater, Okla., n.p. 1967.
MEYERS, JEFFREY. *T. E. Lawrence: A Bibliography.* New York: Garland
Publishing, 1974.

2. Full-length critical studies
FRIEDMAN, JOHN SAUL. "The Challenge of Destiny: A Comparison of T. E.
Lawrence's and Andre Malraux's Adventure Tales." Ph.D. dissertation,
New York University, 1974. Very detailed comparison of Lawrence and
Malraux, who turned the adventure story "into a genre which combines
the *roman d'aventures* with the modern psychological novel."
MEYERS, JEFFREY. *The Wounded Spirit: A Study of "Seven Pillars of
Wisdom".* London: Martin Brian & O'Keeffe, 1973. An excellent,
painstaking literary study which includes comparisons of Lawrence with
Doughty, Nietzsche, and Tolstoy and explains the political and military
background of *Seven Pillars of Wisdom.* Its one fault is that it presses
psychological speculations about Lawrence's "sexual pathology" too far.
O'DONNELL, THOMAS JAMES. "The Dichotomy of Self in T. E. Lawrence's
Seven Pillars of Wisdom." Ph.D. dissertation, University of Illinois at

Urbana-Champaign, 1970. The pioneering critical work on Lawrence as a writer. *Seven Pillars of Wisdom* is analyzed in terms of a masochistic "narrator of introspection" and a dominant "war narrator" and detailed manuscript evidence is used to support this analysis. *The Mint* also receives detailed treatment, and Lawrence is seen as a radical and late representative of the *fin de siècle* artistic tradition. Unusually polished and well-written for a dissertation, its faults are a tendency to bend evidence to fit a somewhat too smooth theory and a lack of knowledge of the Near East.

TABACHNICK, STEPHEN ELY. "T. E. Lawrence's *Seven Pillars of Wisdom* as a Work of Art." Ph.D. dissertation, University of Connecticut, 1971. Absorbed into the present study.

WEINTRAUB, STANLEY, AND WEINTRAUB, RODELLE. *Lawrence of Arabia: The Literary Impulse.* Baton Rouge: Louisiana State University Press, 1975. Semibiographical introduction to Lawrence the writer.

3. Books containing sections of literary interest

ALDINGTON, RICHARD. *Lawrence of Arabia: A Biographical Enquiry.* London: Collins, 1955. An acidulous book, which distorts practically every fact of Lawrence's life but which nontheless contains deep research and penetrating literary comments.

ARMITAGE, FLORA. *The Desert and the Stars.* London: Faber and Faber, 1956. Important as a refutation of Aldington's allegations; substantiates the truth content of Lawrence's autobiographical work.

GRAVES, ROBERT. *Lawrence and the Arabs.* London: Jonathan Cape, 1927. Inaccurate biography, but highly perceptive literary criticism.

KNIGHTLEY, PHILLIP, AND SIMPSON, COLIN. *The Secret Lives of Lawrence of Arabia.* New York: McGraw-Hill, 1970. Far from a definitive biography, but full of source material useful for an understanding of Lawrence as narrator-protagonist of *Seven Pillars* and *The Mint.*

LAWRENCE, A. W., ed. *Letters to T. E. Lawrence.* London: Jonathan Cape, 1962. The best source for detailed, penetrating contemporary criticism of Lawrence's work by Forster, Buchan, the Garnetts, and others.

————, ed. *T. E. Lawrence by his Friends.* New York: McGraw-Hill, 1963. One of the best biographies and full of valuable opinions of Lawrence's work.

MACK, JOHN E. *A Prince of Our Disorder.* London: Weidenfeld and Nicholson, 1976. The most complete, substantial, and trustworthy biography to date.

PAYNE, ROBERT. *Lawrence of Arabia: A Triumph.* London: Hale, 1966. Sometimes inaccurate and sometimes very insightful literary criticism in the context of popularized biography.

RICHARDS, VYVYAN. *A Portrait of T. E. Lawrence.* London: Jonathan Cape, 1936. Excellent source of information about literary influences on Lawrence.

STÉPHANE, ROGER [pseud. of Roger Worms]. *Portrait de l'aventurier: T. E.*

Lawrence, Malraux et von Salomon. Paris: Le Sagittaire, 1950. Valuable as the pioneering comparison of Lawrence and Malraux.

VILLARS, JEAN BERAUD. *T. E. Lawrence Or The Search for the Absolute.* Translated by Peter Dawnay. London: Sidgwick and Jackson, 1958. The most interesting biography to date, including fine literary criticism. Lawrence is seen as the forerunner of political writers such as Malraux, Koestler, and Sartre.

WEINTRAUB, STANLEY. *Private Shaw and Public Shaw.* New York: George Brazillier, 1963. Excellent account of Lawrence's friendship with Mr. and Mrs. G. B. Shaw. It contains very good work on the composition of *Seven Pillars* but gives Shaw far too much credit for revisions.

4. Books on other subjects containing sections of literary interest

BLACKMUR, R. P. "The Everlasting Effort: A Citation of T. E. Lawrence." In *The Lion and the Honeycomb: Essays in Solicitude and Critique.* New York: Harcourt, Brace, 1955. Pp. 97–123. Pioneering attempt to apply the new criticism to *Seven Pillars,* and still one of the most perceptive critiques of the book ever written. Blackmur taxes Lawrence with "forced writing," including strained metaphors, and flat characterization, but places him among the "writers of magnitude" in English literature.

BLYTHE, RONALD. "Sublimated Aladdin." In *The Age of Illusion: England in the Twenties and Thirties 1919–40.* Harmondsworth: Penguin Books, 1964. Pp. 77–98. Lawrence the "arch-romantic for whom fact and fiction were intermingled" as representative of his period.

BUCHAN, JOHN. *Memory Hold-the-Door.* London: Hodder and Stoughton, 1943. Pp. 211–18. Lawrence presented as "a great writer who never quite wrote a great book." *Seven Pillars* seen as a thriller is "shapeless" and "lacks the compulsion of the best narrative" despite some "great moments" of style. *The Mint* is a "tour de force, as astonishing achievement in exact photography" but also a failure because "It lacks relief and half-tones; also shape." Lawrence's *Odyssey* is flawed because "he was not simple-souled enough to translate Homer, so he invented a pre-Raphaelite Homer whom he could translate." The *Letters* are as good as any of Lawrence's books.

CANBY, HENRY. "The Last Great Puritan." In *Seven Years Harvest.* Port Washington, N. Y.: Kennikat Press, 1964. Pp. 40–46. Lawrence's Puritanism "makes his genius so intensely English in its violent nonconformity; it is this which gives blood, as it is Arabia that gives flesh and bones, to his book."

DUNBAR, JANET. "T. E. Lawrence." In *Mrs. G. B. S.: A Portrait.* New York: Harper, 1963. Pp. 231–70. An excellent chapter describing the fascinating relationship between Lawrence and Charlotte Shaw.

FORSTER, E. M. "T. E. Lawrence." In *Abinger Harvest.* London: Edward Arnold, 1936. Pp. 165–71. Excellent criticism of *Seven Pillars,* informed by personal knowledge of Lawrence. Notes that "when he analyses himself it is as a spiritual outcast, on the lines of Herman Melville's Ishmael."

————. "English Prose between 1918 and 1939." *Two Cheers for Democracy*. London: Edward Arnold, 1951. Pp. 280–91. Presents Lawrence as a refugee from industrialism: "it was not by the spear of an Arab but by a high-power motor-bike that he came to his death."

GRAVES, ROBERT. *Goodbye to All That*. Harmondsworth: Penguin Books, 1965. Pp. 242–54. Good background material on the writing of *Seven Pillars* based on personal knowledge.

KNIGHT, G. WILSON. "T. E. Lawrence." In *Neglected Powers*. London: Routledge and Kegan Paul, 1971. Pp. 309–51. An extended comparison of Lawrence and Byron. Knight takes the view that Lawrence *did* understand himself, including his masochistic and homosexual tendencies, and that his chapter "Myself" in *Seven Pillars* is understandable. The last scene in *The Mint* is compared to the work of Powys.

LEWIS, WYNDHAM. "Lawrence of Arabia." In *Blasting and Bombardiering: An Autobiography, 1914–1926*. London: Eyre & Spottiswoode, 1937. Pp. 241–48. Good criticism in the context of the World War I atmosphere by a contemporary writer.

PRITCHETT, V. S. "A Portrait of T. E. Lawrence." In *Books in General*. London; Chatto and Windus, 1953. Pp. 37–42. Reviews David Garnett's *Essential T. E. Lawrence* and constructs a portrait of Lawrence from the selections contained in Garnett's edition. "Hardly classical in manner (for that was "out" in the Twenties and writers were looking for manners which would bring home their nervous singularity) *Seven Pillars* is the solitary classic of the self-conscious warrior, as Doughty is the great self-conscious traveller."

————. "Ross at the Depot." In *The Living Novel & Later Appreciations*. New York: Random House, 1964. Pp. 288–93. Reviews *The Mint* and finds it a failure despite some good passages in Part III. "One is left, at the end of *The Mint*, moved by the writer's pain and nagged by the peculiarity of his case. One is not left with very much more."

READ, HERBERT. "Lawrence of Arabia." In *A Coat of Many Colours: Occasional Essays*. London: Routledge, 1945. Pp. 19–26. "The *Seven Pillars* is a straining after . . . aesthetic grace, and is an artificial monstrosity . . .," but what remains is the "revelation of a man." Lawrence as narrator-protagonist is not an epic hero, as Doughty is.

SPERBER, MANES. "False Situations: T. E. Lawrence and his Two Legends." In *The Achilles Heel*. Translated by Constantine Fitzgibbon. Port Washington, N. Y.: Kennikat Press, 1971. Pp. 175–204. Aldington failed to destroy the "Lawrence legend" because Lawrence *is* a religious figure who takes "himself seriously when describing the quite unnecessary sufferings which he forced himself to undergo."

WILSON, COLIN. "The Attempt to Gain Control." In *The Outsider*. Boston: Houghton Mifflin, 1956. Pp. 71–84. Lawrence searches for his own identity with the help of Puritan discipline and pain, which show him the limits of "his moral freedom."

5. Articles

ALLEN, LOUIS. "French Intellectuals and T. E. Lawrence." *Durham University Journal* 1 (December, 1976), 52–66. Traces the important tradition of French biographies and criticism of Lawrence.

BOAK, DENIS. "Malraux and T. E. Lawrence." *Modern Language Review* 61 no. 2 (1966), 218–24. Malraux saw Lawrence as a "forerunner of Malraux's own vision of the Tragic, man's fight against his destiny and attempt at self-transcendence."

BOWDEN, ANN. "The T. E. Lawrence Collection at the University of Texas." *Texas Quarterly* 5, no. 3 (Autumn, 1962), 54–63. Description of the University of Texas holdings on Lawrence.

FORSTER, E. M. "The Mint," *The Listener*, February 17, 1955, pp. 279–80. A neutral review which reflects Forster's comments to Lawrence himself.

FOSS, MICHAEL. "Dangerous Guides: English Writers and the Desert." *The New Middle East* 9 (June, 1969), 38–42. Excellent comparison of Lawrence with other British poets of Arabian travels; explains Lawrence's underestimation of the Wahabi sect.

GREENLEE, JOHN W. "Malraux, History and Autobiography: *The Seven Pillars of Wisdom* Revisited." *Malraux Miscellany* (1975), 18–35. Malraux's comparison of his own life with Lawrence's.

HARTLEY, L. P. "A Failed Masterpiece." *The Listener*, April 14, 1955, pp. 658–59. Valuable review of *The Mint* by an excellent novelist who finds it admirable but spoiled by abruptness and condensation.

HOWE, IRVING. "T. E. Lawrence: The Problem of Heroism." *Hudson Review* 15 (Autumn, 1962), 333–64. An important article which traces Lawrence's movement from adventure and heroic ideals to a portrayal of "the hero as he appears in the tangle of modern life . . . a man struggling with a vision he can neither realize nor abandon." *Seven Pillars* is a great book, but the *Letters* probably are more accurate autobiography.

HULL, KEITH N. "Creed, History, Prophets and Geography in *Seven Pillars of Wisdom*." *Texas Quarterly* 18(Autumn, 1975), 15–28. Sensible analysis of first seven chapters.

———. "Lawrence of *The Mint*, Ross of the RAF." *South Atlantic Quarterly* 74 (Summer, 1975), 340–48. *The Mint* as biography and art.

———. "T. E. Lawrence's Perilous Parodies." *Texas Quarterly* 2 (Summer, 1972), 56–61. Discusses Tafileh as Lawrence's parody of a battle and a battle report. "Is the true Lawrence the able commander at Tafileh, the sly parodist of the report, or the anguished author of *Seven Pillars* trying desperately to come to grips with his own contradictions? With imperfect sincerity Lawrence was all of these."

KNIGHTLEY, PHILLIP. "Aldington's Enquiry Concerning T. E. Lawrence."

Texas Quarterly 16, no. 4 (Winter, 1973), 98–105. History of the controversy surrounding publication of Aldington's book.

LEWIS, WYNDHAM. "Perspectives on Lawrence." *Hudson Review* 8 (Winter, 1956), 596–608. Refutes Aldington, praises Flora Armitage. *Seven Pillars* is "very well written" and sincere.

MALRAUX, ANDRÉ. "Lawrence and the Demon of the Absolute." *Hudson Review* 8 (Winter, 1956), 519–32. *Seven Pillars* is "not a great narrative," is lacking in characterization, and ends anticlimactically, but is the product of a great religious spirit whose true portrait was "written in the margin."

MEYERS, JEFFREY. "E. M. Forster and T. E. Lawrence: A Friendship." *South Atlantic Quarterly* 69, no. 2 (Spring, 1970), 205–16. Speculates on possibility of homosexuality in this relationship.

———. "Nietzsche and T. E. Lawrence." *Midway* 40, no. 1 (Summer, 1970), 77–85. Included in *The Wounded Spirit*.

———. "The Revisions of *Seven Pillars of Wisdom.*" *Proceeding of the Modern Language Association* 88, no. 5 (October, 1973), 1066–87. Included in *The Wounded Spirit*.

———, "The Secret Lives of Lawrence of Arabia." *Commonweal* 93(October 23, 1970), 100–104. Sharp criticism of the Knightley and Simpson biography.

———. "T. E. Lawrence." *Bulletin of Bibliography* 29 (January–March, 1972), 25–36. Prototype of the Garland Publishing Co. bibliography.

———. "Xenophon and *Seven Pillars,*" *Classical Journal,* 72, 2 (Dec. 1976–Jan. 1977), 141–43. Influence of the *Anabasis* on *Seven Pillars*.

MILLS, GORDON. "T. E. Lawrence as a Writer." *Texas Quarterly* 5, no. 3 (Autumn, 1962), 35–45. A good article which presents Lawrence as a highly conscious stylist, user of motifs and historiographer. Classifies *Seven Pillars* as a work of history and finds it open to a "reasonable understanding."

NOTOPOULOS, JAMES A. "The Tragic and the Epic in T. E. Lawrence." *Yale Review 54, no. 3* (Spring, 1965), 331–45. A highly intelligent and thorough explication of the Homeric parallels in *Seven Pillars* in the light of Lawrence's *Odyssey* translation. Notopoulos sees Lawrence as a "modern figure who experienced the Homeric delirium of the brave and wrote of it with the requisite magic of literature, yet was condemned to tragic frustration by the anachronism of the heroic act in our times."

ROTA, BERTRAM. "Lawrence of Arabia and *Seven Pillars of Wisdom.*" *Texas Quarterly* 5, no. 3 (Autumn, 1962), 46–53. Discussion of identity of "S. A." based on University of Texas manuscripts.

TABACHNICK, STEPHEN ELY. "T. E. Lawrence and *Moby Dick.*" *Research Studies* 44, 1 (March, 1976), 1–12. Lawrence's personality seen in terms of Ahab and Ishmael.

———. "The T. E. Lawrence Revival in English Studies." *Research Studies* 44, no. 3 (September, 1976), 190–98. Review of field as a whole.

————. "Two 'Arabian' Romantics: Charles Doughty and T. E. Lawrence." *English Literature in Transition: 1880–1920* 16, no. 1 (1973), 11–25. Included in the present study.

————. "The Two Veils of T. E. Lawrence." *Studies in the Twentieth Century* 16 (Fall, 1975). Included in the present study.

WEINTRAUB, STANLEY. "Bernard Shaw's Other St. Joan." *South Atlantic Quarterly* 64(Spring, 1965), 194–205. Presents the hypothesis that Lawrence provided the model for Shaw's St. Joan and cites many parallels for evidence.

————, and WEINTRAUB, RODELLE " 'Chapman's Homer.' " *Classical World* (October, 1973), 16–24. Discussion of Lawrence's *Odyssey* translation. Included in *Lawrence of Arabia*.

————. "The Secret Lives of Lawrence of Arabia." *New York Times Book Review*, March 22, 1970, pp. 8, 27. Cautions reader against accepting the Knightley and Simpson biography as definitive but praises them for their apparent identification of "S. A."

Index